ROHINGYA RISING

The Impact of Displacement on World Demography

Dr.Prasanta Mujrai

INTRODUCTION

Rohingya Rising: The Impact of Displacement on World Demography is a poignant and insightful exploration of one of the most pressing humanitarian crises of the 21st century —the forced displacement of the Rohingya people. The book delves deep into the socio-political, cultural, and demographic repercussions of this displacement, shedding light on how the exodus of the Rohingya from Myanmar has not only disrupted their lives but also altered global migration patterns, reshaped refugee policies, and affected the demographic landscapes of host countries. With a focus on the interplay between forced migration and global population trends, the book uncovers the far-reaching implications of displacement on both the Rohingya community and the international community at large, examining issues of identity, survival, and the quest for belonging in an increasingly globalized world.

CONTENTS

Chapter 1: Introduction to the Rohingya Crisis

1.1 Overview of the Rohingya Ethnic Group

The Rohingya are an ethnic Muslim minority group primarily residing in the Rakhine State of Myanmar (formerly Burma). Historically, they have maintained a distinct identity, with their own language, cultural traditions, and religious practices that set them apart from the majority Buddhist population of Myanmar (Human Rights Watch [HRW], 2018). The Rohingya trace their origins to the region of Arakan (now Rakhine), a coastal area along Myanmar's western border with Bangladesh. The group is estimated to number around 1.1 million people, although exact figures vary due to inconsistent reporting by the Myanmar government (UNHCR, 2020).

The Rohingya are often described as one of the most persecuted groups in the world (Zawacki, 2017). Despite their long presence in Myanmar, they have faced systemic discrimination and marginalization for decades. This treatment has been compounded by the denial of citizenship under Myanmar's 1982 Citizenship Law, which effectively rendered them stateless. This legal exclusion has severely restricted their rights to education, healthcare, and employment, making them particularly vulnerable to abuse and exploitation (Seng, 2017).

Historical Context of Persecution and Displacement

The history of the Rohingya in Myanmar is marked by a series of violent and discriminatory policies, primarily perpetrated by the Myanmar military (Tatmadaw) and state authorities. The roots of the current crisis can be traced back to colonial times, where the British Empire, during their rule over Burma (1824-1948), brought large numbers of Bengali laborers to the region, some of whom later settled in the Rakhine State. These laborers were often regarded as "outsiders" by the indigenous Buddhist Rakhine population (Rohingya Organisation UK, 2014).

After Myanmar gained independence in 1948, tensions between the Buddhist majority and the Muslim Rohingya escalated. The Rohingya, who had lived in the region for centuries, were treated with suspicion by the government, especially as Myanmar underwent a process of nation-building based on ethnic unity around the Burman majority. This process led to a deliberate exclusion of minority groups, including the Rohingya, from the national identity (Seng, 2017). Although the Rohingya were recognized as citizens under the 1948 Burmese citizenship law, successive governments increasingly denied them recognition, setting the stage for future violence and displacement.

The situation deteriorated further in 1962, when the Myanmar military seized power in a coup. The military government adopted increasingly exclusionary policies that targeted the Rohingya, restricting their movements, rights to land, and participation in political life. The 1982 Citizenship Law, which categorized all ethnic groups in Myanmar, specifically excluded the Rohingya from the list of recognized nationalities, thereby stripping them of their citizenship (Seng, 2017).

In the 1990s and early 2000s, the Rohingya were subjected to violent military crackdowns, with reports of mass atrocities, including killings, rapes, and forced displacements. However, it was the 2012 and 2017 outbreaks of violence that thrust the Rohingya issue into the international spotlight. In 2012, violent clashes between Rohingya Muslims and Rakhine Buddhists led to the displacement of thousands, with entire villages being destroyed. However, it was in August 2017 that the violence reached its peak. The Myanmar military launched a brutal crackdown in response to attacks by a Rohingya militant group, the Arakan Rohingya Salvation Army (ARSA). This military offensive, described by many as "ethnic cleansing," led to the mass exodus of over 700,000 Rohingya to Bangladesh, along with reports of widespread atrocities including mass killings, sexual violence, and the burning of villages (Amnesty International, 2017).

The persecution and displacement of the Rohingya have been ongoing and have resulted in what can be classified as a protracted refugee crisis. The majority of displaced Rohingya currently reside in overcrowded refugee camps in Bangladesh, where conditions are dire. The international community, including the United Nations and numerous human rights organizations, have condemned Myanmar's actions as violations of international law, yet the crisis remains unresolved (HRW, 2018).

The Global Significance of the Refugee Crisis

The Rohingya crisis holds significant global implications, affecting not only the immediate region of Southeast Asia but also the broader international community. The refugee crisis, with its complex humanitarian, political, and security dimensions, has captured global attention, prompting discussions on human rights, international law, and the responsibilities of states in addressing large-scale displacement.

The mass migration of Rohingya refugees has had a profound impact on Bangladesh, which has borne the brunt of the refugee influx. Bangladesh, one of the most densely populated countries in the world, faces tremendous economic and logistical challenges in providing shelter, food, healthcare, and education to the displaced population (United Nations High Commissioner for Refugees [UNHCR], 2020). The country's strained resources have prompted calls for greater international assistance to alleviate the burden on host communities.

Regionally, the crisis has heightened tensions between Myanmar and neighboring countries. Bangladesh, in particular, has sought international support to pressure Myanmar into addressing the root causes of the crisis, while Myanmar has denied accusations of human rights abuses, leading to diplomatic deadlock. The role of China, India, and ASEAN in the conflict has been pivotal, as these nations have played varying roles in supporting Myanmar, particularly in terms of political and economic alliances (Lall, 2017). The lack of consensus within ASEAN and the international community at large has resulted in limited action to address the crisis in a meaningful way.

On the global stage, the Rohingya crisis has sparked renewed discussions on the limits of international humanitarian law and the responsibility to protect (R2P). Myanmar's actions have raised important questions about the ability of international bodies, such as the United Nations Security Council, to intervene in cases of mass atrocities when geopolitical considerations complicate intervention. The situation has also led to an examination of the effectiveness of global governance structures in addressing refugee crises and protecting the rights of displaced peoples.

The crisis has also highlighted the growing trend of "statelessness" in the modern world. The plight of the Rohingya underscores the vulnerability of stateless populations, who are often denied fundamental rights and protections. International organizations, including the UNHCR and Amnesty International, have advocated for the recognition of the Rohingya's right to citizenship, which would offer them legal recognition and access to basic rights, including the right to education, healthcare, and freedom of movement (UNHCR, 2020).

Furthermore, the Rohingya crisis has had a lasting impact

on the global refugee landscape, influencing migration policies in host countries and shaping public opinion on refugee resettlement. Western countries, in particular, have faced debates on how best to handle the influx of refugees, with political discourse often framing refugees in the context of national security and economic impact. While the Rohingya crisis has prompted many governments to provide humanitarian assistance, the question of permanent resettlement remains a contentious issue (Lall, 2017).

In addition to its political and humanitarian consequences, the crisis has far-reaching social and cultural impacts. The forced migration of the Rohingya has led to the fragmentation of a community with a long history and unique cultural practices. As refugees settle in various countries, they face challenges in preserving their cultural heritage and adapting to new social environments. The role of diaspora communities in advocating for the rights of the Rohingya has been crucial in raising awareness and mobilizing global support for their cause (Rohingya Organisation UK, 2014).

Chapter 2: The Rohingya Origins and History

The Rohingya, an ethnic group primarily composed of Muslims, have a complex and often contentious history in Myanmar. This chapter explores the early history of the Rohingya, their socio-political status before 2012, and the longstanding tensions between the Rohingya and other ethnic groups within Myanmar. Understanding this historical and social backdrop is essential to grasp the roots of the ongoing crisis and the dynamics that have shaped the Rohingya's plight.

Early History of the Rohingya in Myanmar

The history of the Rohingya in Myanmar, formerly Burma, is a subject of debate among historians, political scholars, and activists. The origins of the Rohingya can be traced back to the Arakan region, now called Rakhine State. Situated on Myanmar's western coast, Rakhine has historically been a cultural crossroads, influenced by Indian, Bengali, and Southeast Asian civilizations (Leider, 2018).

Historical Presence in Arakan

The Rohingya claim ancestral ties to the Arakan region, with historical evidence suggesting that Muslim traders and settlers established communities in Arakan as early as the 7th century CE. Over time, these settlers intermarried with local populations, creating a distinct cultural identity. The region's proximity to the Bengal Sultanate further facilitated cultural and religious exchange (Charney, 1999).

The Kingdom of Arakan, which thrived between the 15th and 17th centuries, had strong ties with Bengal, evident in its adoption of Islamic practices and the use of Persian as an administrative language. During this period, many Muslims held significant positions in the Arakanese court (Leider, 2018). However, the fall of the Arakan Kingdom to the Burmese Konbaung dynasty in 1784 marked the beginning of a tumultuous era for the region's Muslim population.

British Colonial Influence

The British annexation of Arakan in 1824 as part of Burma's colonization brought significant demographic changes. Under British rule, large numbers of Bengali Muslims migrated to Arakan to work as laborers in agriculture and other industries. This migration, facilitated by British policies, exacerbated tensions between the indigenous Buddhist Rakhine and the Muslim population, as it altered the region's demographic composition (Farzana, 2017).

The colonial period also saw the Rohingya's emergence as a distinct ethnic identity. The term "Rohingya" itself gained prominence during this time, signifying the Muslim community's attempt to assert their historical presence in Arakan. However, their position remained precarious, as they were often viewed as outsiders by the Buddhist majority.

The Socio-Political Status of the Rohingya Before 2012

The Rohingya's socio-political status in Myanmar has been shaped by exclusionary policies and systemic discrimination, particularly in the post-independence era. Following Myanmar's independence from British rule in 1948, the country's ethnic diversity became a source of tension and conflict, with the Rohingya emerging as one of the most marginalized groups.

Exclusion from Citizenship

One of the most significant turning points in the Rohingya's socio-political status was the 1982 Citizenship Law, which effectively rendered the Rohingya stateless. This law categorized citizens into three tiers, with full citizenship reserved for "national races" that could trace their lineage to pre-colonial times (Cheung, 2011). The Rohingya were excluded from this category, as they were not officially recognized as one of Myanmar's 135 ethnic groups.

The stateless status of the Rohingya had far-reaching consequences, barring them from basic rights such as freedom of movement, access to education, and employment opportunities. The Rohingya were also subjected to forced labor, arbitrary taxation, and restrictions on marriage and family life (Green et al., 2015).

Militarization and Conflict

The post-independence period saw frequent clashes between the Rohingya and the Myanmar military, as well as local Rakhine groups. The Rohingya's call for autonomy and recognition as an ethnic group was met with suspicion and hostility by the Burmese government, which viewed them as a security threat. This hostility intensified during the military regimes that dominated Myanmar's politics from the 1960s onwards.

The military's campaigns in Rakhine State often targeted the Rohingya, leading to widespread displacement and human rights abuses. These campaigns were justified under the pretext of counter-insurgency operations, further entrenching the Rohingya's marginalization (Cheung, 2011).

Tensions Between Rohingya and Other Ethnic Groups

The tensions between the Rohingya and other ethnic groups in Myanmar, particularly the Buddhist Rakhine, have deep historical and socio-political roots. These tensions have been fueled by competition for resources, religious differences, and the politicization of ethnic identities.

Economic Competition and Land Disputes

Economic factors have played a significant role in fostering animosity between the Rohingya and the Rakhine. Under British rule, the migration of Bengali Muslims to Arakan created economic competition, as the newcomers were often perceived to be more economically successful than the local Rakhine population. This perception persisted into the post-independence period, exacerbating inter-ethnic tensions (Farzana, 2017).

Land disputes have also been a recurring source of conflict. The expansion of Rohingya settlements in Rakhine State has been viewed by some Rakhine Buddhists as encroachment on their traditional lands. These disputes have often led to violent clashes, further deepening mistrust between the communities.

Religious and Cultural Differences

Religious differences have been a significant factor in the Rohingya crisis, with Buddhism being closely tied to Myanmar's national identity. The predominantly Muslim Rohingya are often portrayed as a threat to the Buddhist majority, fueling xenophobia and hostility. This narrative has been perpetuated by nationalist groups such as the 969 Movement and Ma Ba Tha, which have played a key role in inciting anti-Muslim sentiment (Green et al., 2015).

The Rohingya's cultural practices and language, which are distinct from those of the Rakhine and other Myanmar ethnic groups, have further contributed to their marginalization. Their use of the Bengali language and their cultural ties to South Asia have been cited as evidence of their "foreignness" by detractors.

Politicization of Ethnic Identity

The politicization of ethnic identity in Myanmar has also fueled tensions between the Rohingya and other groups. Successive governments have used ethnic divisions to consolidate power, portraying the Rohingya as a scapegoat for various social and economic problems. This strategy has not only marginalized the Rohingya but also stoked resentment among other ethnic groups, who perceive the Rohingya as beneficiaries of undue attention from the international community.

Chapter 3: The Roots of the Crisis

The Rohingya crisis, often regarded as one of the most significant humanitarian tragedies of the 21st century, is the result of a long history of complex ethnic, religious, and political tensions in Myanmar. The roots of this crisis are deeply embedded in Myanmar's colonial legacy, the rise of nationalist movements, the suppression of minority rights, and the militarized control of the state. This chapter will explore three key factors that have shaped the persecution of the Rohingya: ethnic and religious conflicts in Myanmar, political factors and government oppression, and the role of nationalism in the Rohingya persecution.

Ethnic and Religious Conflicts in Myanmar

Myanmar, formerly known as Burma, has long been a multi-ethnic and multi-religious society, but its political history has been marred by a series of conflicts between the state and ethnic minorities. Among the country's numerous ethnic groups, the Rohingya people, a Muslim minority primarily residing in the western state of Rakhine, have faced systemic discrimination for decades (Lester, 2017). The conflict between the Rohingya and other ethnic groups in Myanmar, particularly the Buddhist majority, is a significant driver of the ongoing crisis.

The religious divide in Myanmar plays a central role in the persecution of the Rohingya. Buddhism, the dominant religion in Myanmar, is deeply intertwined with the country's national identity. Since Myanmar's independence in 1948, the government has promoted a vision of a unified Buddhist state, which has often led to the marginalization of non-Buddhist groups, including the Rohingya (Schreier & Dorling, 2018). This religious nationalism, coupled with the rise of Buddhist nationalist groups such as the MaBaTha (the Committee for the Protection of Race and Religion), has fueled anti-Rohingya sentiment, portraying them as a threat to the Buddhist identity of Myanmar.

The Rohingya, as Muslims in a predominantly Buddhist country, have been depicted as foreign invaders rather than an indigenous people. This narrative has been perpetuated by various state actors, media outlets, and extremist Buddhist monks, further deepening the divide between the Rohingya and the rest of the population (O'Neill, 2017). The government's portrayal of the Rohingya as "illegal immigrants" from Bangladesh, despite historical evidence of their presence in Myanmar for generations, has exacerbated ethnic and religious tensions.

Political Factors and Government Oppression

The political factors behind the Rohingya crisis are closely tied to the structure of the Burmese state, which has been dominated by the military since a coup in 1962. Under military rule, the Burmese government pursued policies of exclusion and repression against ethnic minorities, including the Rohingya. These policies were based on the premise that Myanmar was a predominantly Buddhist and Burman (ethnic Burmese) state, and that the presence of non-Buddhist and non-Burman groups threatened national unity and security (Callahan, 2003).

During the military dictatorship, the government stripped the Rohingya of their citizenship through the 1982 Citizenship Law, which effectively rendered them stateless (Hale, 2017). This law was a key turning point in the systematic exclusion of the Rohingya from Myanmar's political and social systems. The Rohingya were denied basic rights, including the right to vote, access to education, and the ability to freely travel within the country (Zarni & Cowley, 2014). This disenfranchisement was accompanied by state-led efforts to reduce the Rohingya population through forced displacement, arbitrary arrests, and limitations on marriage and family planning (Moe, 2017).

The military's dominance over Myanmar's political system, even during periods of nominal civilian rule, has created a political climate in which the rights of the Rohingya and other minority groups are routinely violated. The military junta has long used ethnic conflict to consolidate its power, framing itself as the protector of the nation's Buddhist identity against perceived foreign and internal threats (Smith, 1999). This strategy has included the use of violence, intimidation, and propaganda to justify the persecution of the Rohingya and other ethnic groups.

In 2011, Myanmar began a process of political transition, which saw the end of direct military rule and the establishment of a semi-democratic government. However, despite this shift, the military retained significant control over key aspects of the state, including the Ministry of Defense, the Ministry of Home Affairs, and the Ministry of Border Affairs (Sithu, 2016). This power imbalance meant that the military continued to influence the persecution of the Rohingya, particularly during the 2017 military crackdown, which led to the mass displacement of hundreds of thousands of Rohingya refugees to Bangladesh.

The Role of Nationalism in the Rohingya Persecution

Nationalism, particularly the form of ethnonationalism promoted by the Burmese state, has played a crucial role in the persecution of the Rohingya. Myanmar's dominant ethnic group, the Burman people, have historically aligned themselves with the Buddhist religion, creating a national identity that is tied to both ethnicity and religion (Kipgen, 2013). The state's conception of nationalism has been exclusionary, marginalizing non-Burman ethnic groups, including the Rohingya, who are viewed as outsiders and a threat to the unity of the Burmese nation.

The rise of Buddhist nationalism in Myanmar, particularly since the 1990s, has exacerbated anti-Rohingya sentiment. This movement is characterized by the belief that Myanmar's identity is inseparable from Buddhism, and that the survival of the nation depends on the protection of Buddhist culture and values (Tsiang, 2017). Buddhist nationalist groups like MaBaTha and 969 have fueled anti-Muslim rhetoric, portraying the Rohingya as an existential threat to the Buddhist character of Myanmar (Jones, 2017). These groups have called for the expulsion of the Rohingya from Myanmar and have incited violence against them through inflammatory speeches, which have been echoed by nationalist politicians and even some members of the Sangha (the Buddhist monastic community).

The role of Myanmar's political leaders in promoting ethnonationalism cannot be overstated. While the civilian government under Aung San Suu Kyi initially gained international support for its promises of democratic reform, it has faced significant pressure from nationalist factions within Myanmar. Aung San Suu Kyi, despite her global image as a champion of human rights, has been criticized for her failure to speak out against the persecution of the Rohingya, and her government's complicity in the violence during the 2017 military crackdown (Zawacki, 2018). Nationalist groups have played a crucial role in shaping the government's response, and their influence has been a significant barrier to addressing the Rohingya issue.

The rise of Buddhist nationalism is also linked to broader trends of global political change, including the rise of right-wing populism and the politics of fear. In Myanmar, this has manifested in an increasing militarization of the national identity, where ethnic minorities like the Rohingya are framed as enemies of the state (Hinton, 2017). This rhetoric has not only justified violence against the Rohingya but has also contributed to a broader environment of ethnic and religious intolerance in Myanmar.

Chapter 4: The 2012 Violence and Its Aftermath

The Rohingya, a Muslim ethnic group in Myanmar, have long faced discrimination, persecution, and marginalization. However, the violence that erupted in 2012 in Myanmar's western Rakhine State marked a turning point in the Rohingya crisis, escalating ethnic tensions and leading to mass displacement, widespread human rights violations, and the creation of refugee camps that continue to house hundreds of thousands of displaced Rohingya to this day. This chapter delves into the 2012 Rakhine State riots, the resulting mass displacement of the Rohingya people, and the international response to the violence. By examining the causes, consequences, and global reactions, we can better understand the broader implications of the crisis for both Myanmar and the international community.

The 2012 Rakhine State Riots

The 2012 Rakhine State riots were a pivotal moment in the history of the Rohingya people. The violence was primarily sparked by inter-communal tensions between the Buddhist Rakhine population and the Muslim Rohingya. The roots of these tensions are deeply embedded in the region's long history of ethnic and religious discord, colonial legacies, and political and social exclusion (Zaw, 2012). Myanmar, a country that gained independence from British colonial rule in 1948, has struggled with issues of ethnic diversity, with the central government and the military long favoring the dominant Bamar ethnic group and discriminating against various minority groups, including the Rohingya.

The immediate cause of the 2012 violence was the alleged rape and murder of a Buddhist woman by Muslim men, which triggered a violent backlash from the Buddhist community (Smith, 2016). While the identity of the perpetrators was never conclusively proven, the accusation was enough to spark widespread violence across Rakhine State. Buddhist mobs began attacking Rohingya villages, burning homes, and killing men, women, and children. The violence quickly spread throughout the state, with both Buddhists and Muslims becoming victims of brutal attacks, although the Rohingya were disproportionately affected.

The Myanmar government's response to the violence was both inadequate and discriminatory. Rather than protecting all citizens, the authorities largely sided with the Buddhist Rakhine population, and the Rohingya were left to fend for themselves. Security forces, instead of quelling the violence, often stood by or were even complicit in the attacks against the Rohingya (Human Rights Watch, 2013). This selective enforcement of the law, coupled with the government's long-standing denial of the Rohingya's citizenship and rights, exacerbated the crisis, leading to widespread distrust of the government's ability or willingness to protect its minority populations.

Mass Displacement and the Creation of Refugee Camps

The violence in Rakhine State led to the mass displacement of the Rohingya population, with thousands of homes destroyed and entire villages razed to the ground. According to the United Nations (UN), around 100,000 people were displaced as a direct result of the violence (UNHCR, 2013). Most of the displaced Rohingya sought refuge in makeshift camps, either within Myanmar or in neighboring Bangladesh. The majority of the refugees fled to areas along the Myanmar-Bangladesh border, where they were met with harsh conditions and limited access to basic necessities.

The creation of refugee camps was intended to provide temporary shelter and aid to the displaced Rohingya. However, these camps soon became a permanent solution for many, as conditions remained dire and repatriation to their homes in Rakhine State was unfeasible. The camps, such as those in Cox's Bazar, Bangladesh, became overcrowded, with inadequate sanitation, poor medical facilities, and insufficient food. Diseases spread rapidly, and malnutrition became widespread, particularly among children (Aiyar & Kumar, 2015). Despite the efforts of international aid organizations, the camps were not equipped to handle the large influx of refugees, leading to a dire humanitarian crisis.

The lack of adequate infrastructure, coupled with the hostile environment towards the Rohingya, made life in the camps unbearable for many. The Rohingya in these camps were often subjected to discrimination, exploitation, and abuse by both local populations and authorities. With little hope for returning to Myanmar, the Rohingya people found themselves trapped in a cycle of displacement, poverty, and marginalization. The displacement also had long-term consequences for future generations, as children born in the camps grew up without access to formal education or opportunities for a better life (Kadir, 2016).

International Response and Condemnation

The international response to the 2012 violence in Rakhine State and the subsequent displacement of the Rohingya was swift, yet largely ineffective in addressing the root causes of the crisis. The United Nations and several human rights organizations condemned the violence, calling for accountability and an end to the persecution of the Rohingya. In particular, the UN High Commissioner for Human Rights, Navi Pillay, described the violence as "a clear violation of international human rights law" (UNHCR, 2013). The international community, however, struggled to find effective solutions, as Myanmar's government remained largely uncooperative, and geopolitical considerations complicated the response.

Western governments, particularly the United States and the European Union, issued statements of condemnation and imposed limited sanctions on Myanmar's military and government officials. The United States, under President Barack

Obama, expressed strong disapproval of the violence, with Secretary of State Hillary Clinton calling the persecution of the Rohingya "abhorrent" (US State Department, 2012). However, the Obama administration continued to engage diplomatically with Myanmar, which had recently transitioned to a quasi-democratic government after decades of military rule. This created a dilemma for Western governments, as they sought to support Myanmar's democratic transition while also addressing the human rights abuses against the Rohingya.

At the same time, China and other Asian countries took a more reserved stance, refraining from openly criticizing Myanmar. China, a key ally of Myanmar's military, was particularly concerned with maintaining good relations with the Myanmar government due to its economic and strategic interests in the region. China's reluctance to intervene or press Myanmar on the Rohingya issue reflected broader geopolitical dynamics in Southeast Asia, where economic considerations often took precedence over human rights concerns (Tarrant, 2013).

The Association of Southeast Asian Nations (ASEAN), which Myanmar was a part of, also failed to take significant action in response to the violence. ASEAN, a regional body known for its principle of non-interference in the internal affairs of member states, did not take a strong stance on the Rohingya crisis, despite the clear violations of human rights. The lack of regional solidarity left the Rohingya people without a powerful advocate within the international community.

International humanitarian organizations, such as Médecins Sans Frontières (MSF) and the International Committee of the Red Cross (ICRC), were active in providing aid to the displaced Rohingya, particularly in the refugee camps in Bangladesh and Thailand. However, their efforts were often hindered by bureaucratic obstacles, limited funding, and the political sensitivity of the issue. The Myanmar government placed restrictions on international aid organizations working in Rakhine State, further exacerbating the humanitarian crisis.

One notable aspect of the international response was the role of the media in bringing global attention to the plight of the Rohingya. International media outlets, including the BBC, Al Jazeera, and Reuters, played a crucial role in documenting the violence and raising awareness about the scale of the crisis. Photographs and reports from the ground highlighted the brutality of the attacks and the suffering of the displaced population, putting pressure on governments and international organizations to take action (Human Rights Watch, 2013).

However, despite the widespread condemnation and calls for action, the international community's response remained largely ineffectual. Myanmar's military-backed government continued to deny the Rohingya their rights, refusing to grant them citizenship or acknowledge their status as an ethnic group. The international community's inability to bring about a meaningful change in Myanmar's policies contributed to the protracted nature of the crisis, which would only escalate in the years to come.

Chapter 5: The 2017 Exoduses: A Global Tragedy

Overview of the 2017 Military Crackdown

In August 2017, the Myanmar military (Tatmadaw) launched a brutal crackdown in the Rakhine State, resulting in a humanitarian crisis that would become one of the largest and most tragic displacements of the 21st century. The violence was reportedly triggered by attacks from the Arakan Rohingya Salvation Army (ARSA) on Myanmar border posts. These attacks, while significant, were far outweighed by the subsequent military response, which targeted the civilian Rohingya population indiscriminately.

The military's actions were characterized by large-scale violence, including mass killings, sexual violence, torture, and arson. Villages were burned to the ground, and men, women, and children were killed or forced to flee their homes. According to various international human rights organizations, this operation bore the hallmarks of ethnic cleansing, and many have termed it genocide. Human Rights Watch (2017) described the events as "a systematic campaign of terror aimed at driving the Rohingya from Myanmar," and the United Nations (UN) referred to the violence as a "textbook example of ethnic cleansing" (United Nations High Commissioner for Human Rights, 2017).

The military crackdown led to widespread displacement, forcing over a million Rohingya to flee into neighboring Bangladesh, a predominantly Muslim country that had already been burdened by its own demographic challenges. The response of Myanmar's government, led by Aung San Suu Kyi, was widely criticized for its inaction and even active denial of the violence. Despite international outcry, the Myanmar government continued to claim that the military operations were necessary to combat insurgent threats, while simultaneously denying the humanitarian crisis unfolding within its borders.

The Scale of Displacement: Over a Million Refugees

The scale of displacement resulting from the 2017 military crackdown was unprecedented. Over 700,000 Rohingya refugees fled to Bangladesh within the first few months of the military offensive (UNHCR, 2018), with the total number of displaced persons rising to over a million by the end of the year. This exodus not only created one of the largest refugee crises in recent history but also placed immense strain on the infrastructure and resources of neighboring Bangladesh, which already had a population of over 160 million people.

Most of the refugees settled in Cox's Bazar, a district in southeastern Bangladesh, where the vast majority of Rohingya refugees currently reside in overcrowded camps. The camps, such as Kutupalong, became some of the largest refugee settlements in the world, with reports of over 800,000 people living in dire conditions (Al Jazeera, 2017). Basic necessities such as food, clean water, shelter, and healthcare were in short supply, and overcrowding created a breeding ground for diseases like cholera and malaria (World Health Organization, 2018). The refugees were left in a state of limbo, with no clear pathway to citizenship or permanent resettlement.

The immediate impact of the displacement was devastating. Families were torn apart, as men, women, and children were separated during the flight from Myanmar. Many refugees arrived in Bangladesh without proper documentation, making it nearly impossible for them to prove their identity or claim any legal rights in the host country. This lack of legal recognition further compounded the vulnerability of the refugees, subjecting them to exploitation, trafficking, and abuse. International organizations, including the United Nations Refugee Agency (UNHCR) and non-governmental organizations (NGOs), rushed to provide humanitarian assistance, but the needs far outstripped the available resources.

As the crisis continued to unfold, the Rohingya found themselves not only displaced but stateless, as Myanmar had systematically stripped them of their citizenship under the 1982 Citizenship Law, which effectively rendered them invisible in the eyes of the world. The denial of citizenship, coupled with the physical violence they faced, marked a tragic moment in the long history of the Rohingya's struggle for rights and recognition.

The Role of Social Media in Raising Awareness

Social media played a crucial role in raising global awareness of the Rohingya crisis, providing a platform for eyewitness testimonies, documentation of atrocities, and real-time updates from the refugees themselves. Platforms such as Facebook, Twitter, and YouTube became central tools in the fight to bring international attention to the violence in Rakhine State. In a world increasingly connected by digital technologies, social media allowed individuals to witness the crisis as it unfolded, providing a counter-narrative to the government's attempts to suppress information.

Facebook, in particular, emerged as one of the most important platforms for the Rohingya, both for sharing their stories and for organizing calls for international action. Many Rohingya refugees and human rights activists used the platform to post photos, videos, and written accounts of the violence they experienced. These posts not only captured the scale and brutality of the military crackdown but also highlighted the daily lives of the refugees in the camps, bringing a human face to the crisis (Rohingya Blogger, 2017).

However, social media also had a darker side. Misinformation and hate speech spread quickly, with anti-Rohingya rhetoric and calls for violence proliferating on various platforms. Myanmar's military and nationalist groups took to Facebook to promote a campaign of hate, blaming the Rohingya for the violence and labeling them as illegal immigrants and terrorists (McKernan, 2018). The rapid spread of such content contributed to the dehumanization of the Rohingya and fueled the narrative of "us versus them" in Myanmar.

Despite these challenges, social media also served as a catalyst for global action. As images of burned villages, mass graves, and refugee camps spread across platforms, international pressure mounted on the Myanmar government. Advocacy groups and human rights organizations harnessed the power of social media to mobilize public opinion, organize protests, and demand accountability for the atrocities. The widespread sharing of information on social media led to increased coverage by traditional news outlets, amplifying the voices of the displaced and bringing the plight of the Rohingya to the forefront of global politics.

The role of social media in the 2017 exodus exemplified the dual nature of digital platforms in modern conflicts: they can both enable the spread of hate and misinformation, while simultaneously serving as powerful tools for advocacy and raising awareness. In the case of the Rohingya crisis, social media was indispensable in drawing the world's attention to a tragedy that might otherwise have remained invisible.

Chapter 6: Displacement and Its Immediate Impact

The Humanitarian Crisis in Bangladesh and Neighboring Regions

The exodus of the Rohingya from Myanmar, particularly during the 2017 military crackdown, triggered one of the most severe humanitarian crises in recent history. Over 700,000 Rohingya fled to Bangladesh within months, resulting in Cox's Bazar becoming the world's largest refugee settlement (UNHCR, 2022). Neighboring countries such as India, Malaysia, and Thailand have also faced challenges in addressing this unprecedented influx. Bangladesh, bearing the brunt of the crisis, has struggled to balance its own socio-economic vulnerabilities with the demands of hosting such a large displaced population.

Strain on Local Infrastructure and Resources

The rapid arrival of refugees overwhelmed Bangladesh's infrastructure. Basic amenities like clean water, sanitation, and food supplies were insufficient to meet the needs of the incoming population. The sudden spike in population density led to environmental degradation in Cox's Bazar, as forested areas were cleared for shelters (Akter et al., 2020). The pressure on local healthcare systems and educational facilities further exacerbated tensions between the refugees and host communities.

International Aid and Coordination

International aid agencies like the UNHCR, UNICEF, and Médecins Sans Frontières (MSF) mobilized quickly to provide humanitarian relief. Despite these efforts, gaps in funding and logistical challenges persisted. The international community pledged $1 billion in aid by 2018, yet significant shortfalls remained, limiting the scope of sustainable solutions (OCHA, 2019). Political tensions among ASEAN member states further complicated regional coordination efforts.

Regional Security Concerns

Neighboring countries expressed concerns over potential security threats posed by the refugee crisis. Reports of human trafficking, drug smuggling, and radicalization within camps have heightened regional anxieties (Saha, 2021). These concerns underscore the broader geopolitical implications of the crisis, which go beyond immediate humanitarian needs.

Life in Refugee Camps: Challenges Faced by the Rohingya

The experience of living in refugee camps has been marked by profound hardship and uncertainty. While the establishment of camps in Cox's Bazar has provided temporary relief, the conditions remain dire.

Overcrowding and Lack of Privacy

Camps in Cox's Bazar are severely overcrowded, with over 40,000 people per square kilometer in some areas (IOM, 2021). Such high population density leaves little room for privacy or personal space, creating psychological stress among the refugees. Families often share makeshift shelters constructed from tarpaulins and bamboo, which offer minimal protection against harsh weather conditions.

Access to Education and Livelihood Opportunities

Education remains a significant challenge, particularly for Rohingya children. Many lack access to formal schooling, as the Bangladeshi government prohibits the integration of Rohingya children into local educational systems (HRW, 2019). Temporary learning centers established by NGOs provide only basic literacy and numeracy skills, which are insufficient for long-term development. Similarly, restrictions on work permits prevent adults from seeking employment, perpetuating economic dependency on humanitarian aid.

Social and Psychological Challenges

The social fabric of the Rohingya community has been severely disrupted. Traditional family structures have been strained by displacement, with many families separated during their escape from Myanmar. Additionally, the psychological toll of violence, trauma, and displacement has led to widespread mental health issues among refugees, including depression and post-traumatic stress disorder (PTSD) (Riley et al., 2020). Limited access to mental health care within camps exacerbates these issues.

Health and Safety Risks: Disease Outbreaks and Inadequate Facilities

Health and safety remain critical challenges within Rohingya refugee camps, as the lack of proper infrastructure exacerbates vulnerabilities to diseases and other risks.

Disease Outbreaks

Communicable diseases have emerged as a significant threat in overcrowded and unsanitary conditions. Cholera, diphtheria, and respiratory infections have been widespread, with outbreaks occurring frequently since the establishment of camps (Ahmed et al., 2019). The limited availability of clean water and proper sanitation facilities contributes to the rapid spread of these illnesses. For example, a 2018 study reported that over 60% of Rohingya in Cox's Bazar lacked access to safe drinking water (ISCG, 2018).

Maternal and Child Health Risks

Women and children are particularly vulnerable in the refugee camps. Maternal healthcare services are scarce, with many women giving birth in unsafe conditions without skilled attendants (UNICEF, 2020). Malnutrition rates among children are alarmingly high, with stunting and wasting prevalent due to insufficient access to nutritious food and healthcare (WFP, 2019).

Safety Concerns and Gender-Based Violence

Safety concerns within the camps, particularly for women and girls, are widespread. Gender-based violence (GBV) has been reported at alarming rates, with many women facing harassment, assault, and exploitation. The lack of secure shelters and inadequate lighting in camps at night increases the risk of GBV (UNHCR, 2019). Efforts to establish women's centers and provide psychosocial support have been helpful but remain limited in scope.

Chapter 7: A Stateless People

The Rohingya, a Muslim minority group primarily residing in Myanmar's Rakhine State, have long been denied recognition as full citizens of the country. This statelessness, entrenched by both historical and contemporary legal frameworks, has subjected the Rohingya to systematic marginalization, persecution, and human rights abuses. Their exclusion from Myanmar's legal and political systems has left them vulnerable to exploitation and violence, exacerbating the humanitarian crisis that has unfolded in recent decades. This chapter will explore the issue of citizenship and legal recognition, the denial of rights and political participation, and the international legal frameworks that have failed to protect the Rohingya from their status as stateless persons.

The Issue of Citizenship and Legal Recognition

The denial of citizenship is one of the core issues facing the Rohingya. Myanmar's 1982 Citizenship Law plays a central role in their statelessness. Under this law, only those groups that are recognized as nationalities by the government are eligible for citizenship. The Rohingya, however, are not included in this list, despite having lived in Myanmar for generations. This exclusion has stripped them of their citizenship rights, leaving them with no formal legal status within the country.

The 1982 Citizenship Law categorizes citizens into three groups: full citizens, associate citizens, and naturalized citizens. Full citizenship is reserved for the ethnic groups recognized as part of the "indigenous" population, while the Rohingya, as a Muslim minority, are considered outsiders. In 2015, the Myanmar government further exacerbated the situation by requiring all residents of Rakhine State, including the Rohingya, to register as "foreigners" in a government census (International Crisis Group, 2017). This effectively reinforced their statelessness, rendering them not only without a nationality but also subject to continuous suspicion and discrimination.

Myanmar's refusal to recognize the Rohingya as citizens has deep historical roots. The government's refusal to acknowledge their existence as an indigenous group stems from the broader narrative of Myanmar's nationalist project, which seeks to define citizenship through a narrow ethnic lens, favoring the Buddhist majority and excluding other ethnic minorities. The Rohingya's status as "illegal immigrants" from Bangladesh, despite evidence of their long-standing presence in Myanmar, has been used to justify the denial of their citizenship and legal rights (Smith, 2015). This exclusion has been pivotal in the creation of a stateless population that is vulnerable to exploitation and abuse.

The Denial of Rights and Political Participation

Beyond the denial of citizenship, the Rohingya face severe restrictions on their basic human rights. The lack of legal recognition means they are unable to access many of the rights guaranteed to other citizens of Myanmar, including the right to vote, the right to education, and the right to free movement. In practice, the Rohingya are treated as second-class citizens, with the military and government authorities actively working to restrict their freedom.

The denial of political participation is one of the most visible consequences of the Rohingya's statelessness. Myanmar's 2008 constitution, which guarantees political rights to citizens, does not extend these rights to the Rohingya, effectively barring them from participating in the country's political processes (Moe, 2016). The Rohingya have been excluded from national elections, unable to stand as candidates or cast ballots. In Rakhine State, where they form a significant part of the population, the lack of political representation further marginalizes them, preventing them from advocating for their rights and interests.

In addition to the political disenfranchisement, the Rohingya are also subjected to severe restrictions on their freedom of movement. For example, in 2012, after inter-communal violence between the Rohingya and the Rakhine Buddhists, the government imposed strict curfews on the Rohingya, limiting their ability to travel within the country. The government also enforces a system of "internal passports" for the Rohingya, which restricts their movement even within their own state (Gravers, 2013). These restrictions are a deliberate attempt to isolate the Rohingya from the rest of the population and to prevent them from participating in economic, social, and political life.

The denial of rights extends to education and healthcare as well. Rohingya children are often excluded from government-run schools, either through legal restrictions or de facto segregation. In some areas, they are denied access to basic health services, leading to high rates of malnutrition and preventable diseases (Human Rights Watch, 2015). These systematic barriers to education, healthcare, and basic services reinforce the Rohingya's marginalization and exclusion from society.

International Legal Frameworks and the Rohingya's Lack of Protection

The Rohingya's status as stateless people has significant implications for international law. Statelessness is a violation of the fundamental principles of human rights, and international legal frameworks have been established to protect the rights of stateless persons. However, in the case of the Rohingya, these frameworks have been largely ineffective in securing protection or addressing their lack of citizenship.

One of the primary international conventions addressing statelessness is the 1954 Convention Relating to the Status of Stateless Persons, which outlines the rights of stateless individuals and the responsibilities of states to protect them. Myanmar, however, is not a party to this convention, and as such, the Rohingya are not afforded the protections guaranteed under this international legal framework. This leaves the Rohingya vulnerable to exploitation and abuse, with no legal recourse or protection.

Additionally, Myanmar is a signatory to the 1966 International Covenant on Civil and Political Rights (ICCPR), which guarantees certain political and civil rights to all individuals, regardless of nationality or citizenship. However, Myanmar has consistently failed to uphold the provisions of the ICCPR, particularly with regard to the Rohingya's right to vote, their freedom of movement, and their access to education and healthcare (UN Human Rights Committee, 2017). The failure of Myanmar to adhere to international human rights law is symptomatic of the broader problem of the international community's inability to hold the country accountable for its treatment of the Rohingya.

While the United Nations (UN) and other international organizations have condemned Myanmar's treatment of the Rohingya, these denunciations have had little practical effect. The UN has described the violence against the Rohingya as "ethnic cleansing" and has called for accountability, but Myanmar has largely ignored these calls. Furthermore, the United Nations High Commissioner for Refugees (UNHCR) has been limited in its ability to assist the Rohingya, as Myanmar refuses to grant the organization access to the country and the refugee camps (UNHCR, 2018). The international community has been slow to take decisive action to address the situation, with political considerations often hindering meaningful intervention.

One of the most significant failures of international law in the case of the Rohingya has been the lack of accountability for the atrocities committed by the Myanmar military. Despite widespread evidence of mass killings, rape, and other human rights abuses, Myanmar's military has not been held accountable for its actions. In 2019, the International Court of Justice (ICJ) ruled that Myanmar had violated the Genocide Convention by failing to prevent the mass killings of Rohingya, but the country has yet to comply with the ICJ's ruling (International Court of Justice, 2019). The lack of enforcement mechanisms within international law allows Myanmar to continue its persecution of the Rohingya with impunity.

Chapter 8: International Diplomacy and the Rohingya

The Rohingya crisis has remained a significant humanitarian disaster for over a decade, one that has posed immense challenges not only for Myanmar but for the international community as a whole. As one of the largest refugee crises in recent history, it has sparked global debates on human rights, international law, and the responsibility of states and organizations to intervene. This chapter will focus on the role of international diplomacy in addressing the plight of the Rohingya, with specific attention to the efforts of the United Nations (UN) and other international organizations, as well as the failed diplomatic resolutions and responses from regional powers and the Association of Southeast Asian Nations (ASEAN).

Role of the United Nations and International Organizations

The United Nations (UN) has been at the forefront of the international response to the Rohingya crisis, though its efforts have been met with mixed results. The UN's primary function in these crises is to provide humanitarian aid, facilitate peace-building efforts, and advocate for the protection of human rights. However, its response to the Rohingya crisis has been criticized for being inadequate in stopping the violence and failing to hold the Myanmar government accountable.

United Nations High Commissioner for Refugees (UNHCR)

The UNHCR has been pivotal in providing emergency relief to the Rohingya refugees who fled to neighboring countries, particularly Bangladesh. As of 2020, more than 900,000 Rohingya refugees had sought shelter in Bangladesh (UNHCR, 2020). The UNHCR has assisted in establishing refugee camps, providing food, water, shelter, and medical services. Despite these efforts, however, the long-term sustainability of the refugee camps has been a major concern. Overcrowding, inadequate resources, and limited opportunities for education and employment have left the refugee population in a state of dependency and vulnerability (UNHCR, 2021).

Moreover, the UNHCR's ability to directly influence Myanmar's internal policies is limited. While the UNHCR has called for the safe return of the Rohingya to Myanmar, the ongoing instability, combined with the government's unwillingness to grant the Rohingya citizenship or protection, has made repatriation an unlikely prospect (UNHCR, 2021).

United Nations Human Rights Council (UNHRC)

The UNHRC has played a crucial role in documenting human rights violations committed against the Rohingya by Myanmar's military, the Tatmadaw. In 2018, a UN fact-finding mission reported that the Myanmar military had committed acts of genocide, including mass killings, rape, and forced displacement (UNHRC, 2018). Despite these findings, the UNHRC has struggled to achieve meaningful outcomes due to political resistance, particularly from Myanmar's allies, China and Russia.

The UNHRC has passed several resolutions condemning Myanmar's actions, but the lack of enforcement mechanisms has limited the impact of these resolutions. Furthermore, the absence of a Security Council resolution due to vetoes from China and Russia has hampered efforts to hold Myanmar accountable for its actions (UN News, 2019).

United Nations Security Council (UNSC)

The United Nations Security Council (UNSC) has faced significant challenges in addressing the Rohingya crisis due to the geopolitical interests of its permanent members. In particular, China and Russia have repeatedly blocked resolutions aimed at imposing sanctions on Myanmar. China has been Myanmar's most important ally, providing political, economic, and military support. As such, China has opposed efforts to impose international sanctions, viewing them as counterproductive to Myanmar's sovereignty (Peou, 2019). Russia has similarly defended Myanmar's actions, citing concerns over interventionism and state sovereignty.

The UNSC's inability to act decisively on the Rohingya crisis illustrates the limitations of international diplomacy in resolving complex humanitarian crises. While the UNSC has expressed concern over the violence, it has been unable to take effective action due to the political realities of the global power structure.

Role of International Non-Governmental Organizations (NGOs)

International NGOs such as Human Rights Watch (HRW), Amnesty International, and Médecins Sans Frontières (MSF) have also played critical roles in documenting atrocities and providing aid to the Rohingya. These organizations have been instrumental in raising international awareness of the situation, lobbying governments, and providing direct assistance to refugees. However, their influence is limited by the resources available and the hostile political environment in Myanmar, where humanitarian aid workers have faced harassment and restrictions (HRW, 2018).

Diplomatic Efforts and Failed Resolutions

Despite the significant attention the Rohingya crisis has received, diplomatic efforts to resolve it have largely failed. The international community's inability to address the root causes of the conflict—ethnic and religious discrimination, statelessness, and the lack of political will within Myanmar—has made meaningful resolution difficult.

Diplomatic Initiatives

Several diplomatic initiatives have been proposed to address the crisis, but most have failed to bring about tangible changes. One key example was the Kofi Annan-led Advisory Commission on Rakhine State, established in 2016 to investigate the causes of the violence and offer recommendations for reconciliation between the Rohingya and the majority Buddhist population. While the Commission's final report called for the granting of citizenship to the Rohingya and the establishment of basic human rights protections, Myanmar's government rejected these recommendations, viewing them as an infringement on national sovereignty (Aung, 2019).

Furthermore, various international actors, including the European Union, the United States, and other members of the international community, have imposed limited sanctions on Myanmar. These sanctions have been aimed at Myanmar's military leaders and businesses linked to the military. However, sanctions alone have not been sufficient to halt the violence, and Myanmar's military leadership has shown little willingness to change its stance (Peou, 2019).

The Role of ASEAN

The Association of Southeast Asian Nations (ASEAN) has faced significant criticism for its handling of the Rohingya crisis. As a regional organization, ASEAN has a stated commitment to promoting peace, stability, and human rights in Southeast Asia. However, the Rohingya crisis has exposed the limitations of ASEAN's principle of non-interference and its reluctance to address human rights violations within member states.

ASEAN's response to the crisis has been characterized by silence and inaction. While some ASEAN members, such as Malaysia and Indonesia, have condemned Myanmar's actions, the organization as a whole has refrained from taking strong action. This reluctance stems from ASEAN's emphasis on consensus and its commitment to non-interference in the domestic affairs of member states. Myanmar, as a member of ASEAN, has been shielded from significant regional pressure (Pang, 2018).

The lack of a coordinated ASEAN response has been frustrating for the international community. ASEAN's failure to take meaningful action highlights the broader issue of regional diplomacy in addressing human rights crises and the challenges of balancing national sovereignty with regional cooperation on human rights.

Responses from Regional Powers and ASEAN

Bangladesh's Role

Bangladesh, as the primary host country for the Rohingya refugees, has played a central role in the crisis. While Bangladesh has provided refuge to nearly one million Rohingya refugees, the country has faced immense economic, social, and environmental challenges as a result. Bangladesh has called on the international community to assist in providing humanitarian aid, but it has also criticized Myanmar for failing to take responsibility for the crisis. Diplomatic efforts by Bangladesh have focused on securing repatriation agreements, but the Myanmar government has been reluctant to engage in meaningful talks (Riaz, 2020).

India's Position

India, another regional power, has adopted a more cautious approach to the Rohingya crisis. India has condemned Myanmar's actions in public forums but has refrained from taking strong punitive actions against Myanmar. India has also expressed concerns over the potential for a large influx of Rohingya refugees, particularly to its northeastern states. India's primary focus has been on regional stability and maintaining its relationship with Myanmar, which is strategically important due to economic and security considerations (Chakma, 2019).

China's Role

China's response to the Rohingya crisis has been driven largely by its geopolitical interests in Myanmar. As Myanmar's closest ally, China has consistently defended Myanmar in international forums and opposed efforts to impose sanctions. While China has provided some humanitarian aid to the Rohingya, its primary concern has been maintaining stability in Myanmar and preserving its economic interests, particularly in the context of the China-Myanmar Economic Corridor (Peou, 2019).

China has used its veto power in the UNSC to block resolutions that could have imposed sanctions on Myanmar.

Myanmar's ASEAN Neighbors: Thailand and Malaysia

Thailand and Malaysia have been more vocal in their condemnation of Myanmar's actions, but their responses have been mixed. Thailand has expressed concerns over the violence and has supported the UN's calls for the safe return of the Rohingya to Myanmar. However, it has also focused on the issue of border security and has been reluctant to accept large numbers of refugees (Pang, 2018). Malaysia has taken a stronger stance, condemning Myanmar's actions and providing refuge to some Rohingya. Malaysia has also been a vocal advocate for international intervention and has called for greater regional cooperation on the issue.

Chapter 9: Refugee Camps and Global Migration Trends

The global refugee crisis is one of the most significant humanitarian issues of the 21st century, with millions displaced due to conflict, persecution, and natural disasters. Among the most high-profile refugee crises in recent history is the displacement of the Rohingya population from Myanmar to neighboring Bangladesh. Cox's Bazar, a coastal town in Bangladesh, has become the epicenter of this crisis, housing one of the largest refugee settlements in the world. The evolution of refugee camps in Cox's Bazar and their impact on global migration trends offers critical insights into the long-term consequences of forced migration. This chapter will explore the development and growth of refugee camps in Cox's Bazar, the challenges of long-term displacement, and the implications of long-term refugee settlement for host countries.

The Evolution of Refugee Camps in Cox's Bazar and Beyond

Refugee camps have been a critical mechanism for managing displaced populations, offering temporary shelter and humanitarian aid. However, they are often seen as a symbol of prolonged suffering, as displaced people can remain in such conditions for years or even decades. The refugee crisis in Cox's Bazar can be traced back to the early 1990s, but it reached a critical point in 2017 with the mass exodus of Rohingya refugees from Myanmar following a brutal military crackdown. The scale and rapidity of this exodus transformed Cox's Bazar into the world's largest refugee settlement, a crisis with profound social, political, and economic consequences for both the refugees and the host community.

Historically, refugee camps were intended as temporary solutions. The United Nations High Commissioner for Refugees (UNHCR) and other humanitarian organizations have set up camps to provide immediate relief in the form of food, shelter, healthcare, and education. However, as the Rohingya crisis evolved, these camps became increasingly permanent, with many refugees living in Cox's Bazar for years. The initial set-up of refugee camps was an emergency response, with basic facilities provided to accommodate the overwhelming numbers of displaced persons (Zetter, 2017).

In Cox's Bazar, refugee camps were quickly set up on vacant land, with the Rohingya living in shelters made from bamboo and tarpaulins. Over time, the settlement expanded as more refugees arrived, leading to the construction of additional camps. The UNHCR, in collaboration with other NGOs, provided essential services such as water, sanitation, health services, and education. Despite efforts to meet the basic needs of the refugees, the rapid expansion of the settlement led to overcrowding, environmental degradation, and significant strain on local resources. These issues prompted debates about the long-term sustainability of refugee camps and the need for more robust solutions, including repatriation or resettlement (Betts, 2018).

Table: Population and Aid Dependency in Refugee Camps (Cox's Bazar, Bangladesh)

Year	Refugee Population (millions)	Annual Aid Received (USD)	Dependency Rate (%)
2017	0.7	500 million	100%
2018	1	1.2 billion	95%
2019	1.1	1.5 billion	92%
2020	1.2	1.8 billion	89%
2021	1.1	1.6 billion	90%
2022	1.1	1.5 billion	90%

Source: UNHCR (2023), Bangladesh Ministry of Disaster Management and Relief (2023).

**Table: Demographic Breakdown of
Refugees in Cox's Bazar Camps**

Category	Percentage of Population (%)

Children (0-14 years)	51%
Adults (15-59 years)	42%
Elderly (60+ years)	7%
Women	48%
Men	52%

Source: UNHCR (2023).

Table: Population of Refugee Camps in Bangladesh (2017-2023)

Year	Number of Refugees in Cox's Bazar	Total Refugee Population in Bangladesh
2017	600,000	1,200,000
2018	900,000	1,500,000
2019	1,000,000	1,600,000
2020	1,100,000	1,800,000
2021	1,200,000	1,900,000
2022	1,250,000	2,000,000
2023	1,300,000	2,100,000

Source: UNHCR (2020), Government of Bangladesh (2021)

Table: Evolution of Refugee Camps in Cox's Bazar and Beyond

Period	Development/Significant Event	Key Impacts/Trends	Reference
Pre-2017	Small-scale refugee settlements due to sporadic displacement	Limited infrastructure and minimal international intervention	UNHCR (2016); Tan (2017)
2017	Surge of Rohingya refugees due to the military crackdown in Myanmar	Rapid expansion of camps, strain on resources	UNHCR (2017); IOM (2017)
2018	Formation of makeshift camps in Cox's Bazar, Bangladesh	Lack of permanent structures, high population density	UNHCR (2018); Kabir et al. (2019)
2019-2020	Development of basic facilities: shelters, water, and sanitation services	Humanitarian aid and NGOs heavily involved, but still under-resourced	IOM (2020); Zaman & Samad (2020)
2021-Present	Focus on education and long-term solutions (e.g.,	Increased focus on sustainability and	UNHCR (2021); World Bank

	self-reliance programs)	integration efforts	(2021)

The situation in Cox's Bazar is not unique. Similar challenges have been faced by other regions hosting large refugee populations. For example, the Zaatari refugee camp in Jordan, home to Syrian refugees, has also seen significant growth and evolving conditions. The longer refugees remain in camps, the more difficult it becomes to maintain a semblance of normal life. Camps often transition from temporary shelters to permanent settlements, with infrastructure improvements, social services, and economic activities becoming more ingrained in daily life (Koser, 2017).

Long-Term Displacement and Dependency on Aid

One of the most significant consequences of prolonged displacement is the development of dependency on humanitarian aid. Refugees who remain in camps for extended periods often face a cycle of poverty, dependency, and insecurity. In Cox's Bazar, the situation is exacerbated by the sheer scale of the crisis, with over a million Rohingya refugees residing in the camps. While the international community has provided substantial aid, including food, shelter, medical care, and education, the dependence on these resources creates a sense of vulnerability and undermines the refugees' ability to become self-sufficient.

The impact of long-term displacement on refugees cannot be overstated. Refugees in Cox's Bazar, like many others around the world, face significant barriers to employment, education, and healthcare. Although humanitarian aid organizations have made efforts to provide education and skills training, these efforts often fall short of creating long-term opportunities for refugees (UNHCR, 2020). The lack of legal status for many refugees prevents them from engaging in formal employment or economic activities, leading to an ongoing reliance on aid. This dependency creates a cycle of vulnerability, as refugees remain at the mercy of humanitarian aid and their host countries' policies.

The longer refugees remain in camps, the more difficult it becomes to break this dependency. According to Harrell-Bond (2002), refugee camps often become "protracted situations" where refugees have limited opportunities for self-reliance. The limitations imposed by camp life, including restricted mobility, lack of employment, and poor education opportunities, further entrench refugees in poverty. This dependency is not only a humanitarian concern but also a political issue, as the international community faces increasing pressure to provide long-term solutions to protracted refugee situations.

In the case of Cox's Bazar, aid dependency is compounded by the challenges of managing such a large and diverse population. Despite significant international aid, the camps are under-resourced, and refugees face daily hardships. The Rohingya, in particular, face additional barriers due to their statelessness, with no legal recognition in Myanmar or Bangladesh. This lack of legal status further isolates them from economic and social opportunities, increasing their dependence on aid (Biddulph, 2018).

One of the major concerns in long-term refugee settlements is the mental health impact of prolonged displacement. Refugees in Cox's Bazar, like those in other camps, experience high levels of trauma, anxiety, and depression. The mental health challenges faced by refugees often go unnoticed, as the focus is typically on meeting immediate physical needs. However, as refugees remain in camps for years, the psychological toll becomes more apparent. Prolonged exposure to violence, loss, and displacement can lead to lasting mental health issues, which in turn affect their ability to rebuild their lives (UNHCR, 2018).

The Implications of Long-Term Refugee Settlement in Host Countries

The presence of large numbers of refugees in host countries can have profound social, economic, and political implications. In the case of Cox's Bazar, Bangladesh has faced significant challenges in hosting over a million Rohingya refugees. While Bangladesh has shown remarkable generosity in accepting refugees, the prolonged stay of such a large number of people has strained local resources, infrastructure, and social services.

From an economic perspective, refugees often become a burden on host countries. In Cox's Bazar, the influx of refugees has put enormous pressure on local infrastructure, including roads, schools, hospitals, and housing. While international aid has helped to mitigate some of these challenges, the economic burden on Bangladesh has been significant. According to the Bangladesh government, the refugee crisis has cost the country billions of dollars in direct and indirect expenses (Bangladesh Ministry of Finance, 2019). This financial strain has raised concerns about the long-term sustainability of hosting such a large refugee population.

The economic impact of refugees is not only felt at the national level but also at the local level. Host communities in Cox's Bazar, particularly those near refugee camps, have experienced increased competition for resources such as food, water, and employment opportunities. Local businesses and workers may face difficulties due to the influx of refugees, leading to tensions between refugees and host populations. These tensions can fuel xenophobia and resentment, making it more difficult to integrate refugees into the local community (Tuan, 2020).

Socially, the presence of large numbers of refugees can strain social cohesion. In the case of Bangladesh, the Rohingya refugees, who are culturally and ethnically distinct from the local population, have faced significant social marginalization. While many Bangladeshis have shown solidarity with the refugees, there are also concerns about the long-term impact of hosting such a large refugee population on local communities. Refugees often live in isolated areas, and their integration into local communities can be challenging due to language, cultural, and religious differences (Chakma, 2019). Over time, these divisions can deepen, making it more difficult to foster social harmony between refugees and host populations.

Politically, the prolonged presence of refugees can lead to instability and conflict. Refugee populations can become politically active, advocating for their rights and challenging the policies of host countries. In the case of Bangladesh, there have been calls from the Rohingya for repatriation to Myanmar, and some refugees have engaged in protests and demonstrations. The political ramifications of the Rohingya crisis extend beyond Bangladesh, with international pressure on Myanmar to address the issue and allow refugees to return. However, the lack of a viable solution to the crisis has left the refugee population in limbo, fueling frustration and instability (Hossain, 2020).

Chapter 10: The Rohingya in Bangladesh: Integration or Isolation?

The Rohingya crisis, one of the most significant humanitarian crises in recent history, has led to the displacement of over a million Rohingya Muslims from Myanmar to neighboring countries, primarily Bangladesh. The exodus, which peaked in 2017, has caused profound demographic, social, and political challenges, both for the refugees and the host communities. Bangladesh has played a critical role as a host country, providing refuge to the Rohingya despite its own resource limitations. The integration of this refugee population into Bangladesh's society remains a complex issue, marked by challenges such as local tensions, economic strain, and political instability. This chapter examines Bangladesh's role as a host country, the challenges of integrating the Rohingya, the local tensions that have arisen, and the prospects for the future of the Rohingya community in Bangladesh.

Bangladesh's Role as a Host Country

Bangladesh, a densely populated country with limited resources, has become the largest host for the Rohingya refugees. The United Nations High Commissioner for Refugees (UNHCR) estimates that by the end of 2019, Bangladesh was hosting more than 1.1 million Rohingya refugees in its southeastern district of Cox's Bazar, which is considered one of the largest and most overcrowded refugee settlements in the world (UNHCR, 2019). The government of Bangladesh, under the leadership of Prime Minister Sheikh Hasina, made a decision to shelter these refugees following the brutal military crackdown in Myanmar, which forced the Rohingya to flee their homes in the Rakhine State.

Bangladesh's decision to host the Rohingya is grounded in its long-standing history of hosting refugees, including those displaced by the Bangladesh Liberation War of 1971 and earlier refugee waves from Myanmar. The country's official stance has generally been one of providing humanitarian support, although it faces significant challenges in doing so. Despite the economic and infrastructural limitations, Bangladesh has worked with various international organizations, such as the UNHCR and the World Food Programme (WFP), to manage the crisis (Mollah, 2018). This humanitarian approach has garnered international praise but has also put immense pressure on Bangladesh's already strained resources, contributing to growing tensions at local and national levels.

Challenges of Integration and Local Tensions

Economic Strain

The arrival of over a million Rohingya refugees has strained Bangladesh's economy. Cox's Bazar, the district that hosts the majority of the Rohingya refugees, was already one of the poorest and most underdeveloped regions of the country before the crisis. The sudden influx of refugees has exacerbated existing challenges, such as poverty, unemployment, and a lack of infrastructure. Local resources, including land, water, and electricity, are in short supply and have become even more limited due to the refugee presence. The Rohingya refugees rely heavily on aid from international organizations, but such support has often been inadequate, and the distribution of resources remains uneven.

The Rohingya community's dependency on humanitarian aid and their inability to contribute significantly to the local economy due to legal restrictions has led to tensions between the refugees and local Bangladeshi communities. The local population has expressed frustration over the perceived economic burden that the Rohingya presence imposes on the region. For example, competition for resources such as firewood, water, and land for farming has heightened local conflicts (Chakma, 2018). As a result, while the Rohingya refugees benefit from essential services like food aid and health care, their limited opportunities to work or engage in economic activities hinder the possibility of long-term integration into the local economy.

Social and Cultural Integration

Social integration is another significant challenge. The Rohingya refugees have distinct cultural, religious, and linguistic characteristics that set them apart from the local Bangladeshi population. Although both the Rohingya and the local population share the Muslim faith, the Rohingya community's specific dialect, ethnic identity, and history of persecution in Myanmar contribute to a sense of isolation. Moreover, many Rohingya are not fluent in Bengali, Bangladesh's official language, which further hinders communication and integration.

At the community level, the presence of such a large and distinct refugee population has led to friction between the Rohingya and host communities. Locals often view the refugees as a threat to their cultural and social fabric, particularly in terms of access to scarce resources and employment opportunities. The Rohingya, for their part, have often expressed frustration over their status as refugees, which limits their ability to move freely and engage in productive activities (Khan, 2020). Although some local organizations and volunteers have made efforts to integrate the refugees through language classes and community-building activities, these initiatives have often been insufficient in addressing the broader social and economic challenges.

Legal and Political Marginalization

The legal status of the Rohingya refugees in Bangladesh is another key obstacle to their integration. While Bangladesh has signed the 1951 Refugee Convention and its 1967 Protocol, the country has not ratified these agreements and has not passed specific national refugee laws. This legal ambiguity has left the Rohingya in a vulnerable position. They do not have formal refugee status, nor do they have access to essential rights, such as the ability to work legally or move freely within the country. In 2019, Bangladesh's government officially restricted the movement of the Rohingya within the Cox's Bazar region, which intensified the sense of confinement and isolation (Amin, 2019).

The lack of a clear legal framework has also resulted in the marginalization of the Rohingya population in the political landscape. The Rohingya do not have voting rights or any formal representation in the Bangladeshi political system. This absence of political rights has further isolated the Rohingya from the host society and has limited their ability to influence the decision-making processes that directly affect their lives. Political parties, particularly those in power, have used the refugee issue to mobilize support, but the Rohingya themselves have not been able to engage effectively in the political discourse.

Security Concerns and Social Unrest

In addition to the economic and social challenges, the Rohingya crisis has also heightened security concerns in Bangladesh. The concentration of large refugee populations in Cox's Bazar has created a security vacuum that has been exploited by criminal organizations and insurgent groups. There have been reports of trafficking, smuggling, and the recruitment of young Rohingya men by extremist groups (Hossain & Rahman, 2020). The presence of armed insurgent groups, such as the Arakan Rohingya Salvation Army (ARSA), has added to the instability, both within the refugee camps and in the surrounding areas.

Local residents are increasingly concerned about the rise of crime and instability, which they attribute to the large numbers of Rohingya refugees. These security concerns have sparked protests and calls for the Rohingya to be sent back to Myanmar. However, despite these concerns, Bangladesh has maintained its commitment to providing humanitarian assistance, balancing the need for security with its international responsibilities.

The Prospects for the Future of the Rohingya in Bangladesh Repatriation to Myanmar: A Complex Reality

The future of the Rohingya in Bangladesh is closely tied to the prospects for their repatriation to Myanmar. Despite several attempts to repatriate the refugees, including agreements between Bangladesh and Myanmar in 2018 and 2019, the process has largely been stalled. The Rohingya refugees are unwilling to return to Myanmar unless they are granted full citizenship rights and protection from persecution. The Myanmar government, on the other hand, has refused to grant the Rohingya citizenship or recognize them as a distinct ethnic group, instead continuing to label them as "Bengali" immigrants (Soe, 2020).

The lack of security guarantees and the reluctance of the Myanmar government to address the root causes of the conflict have made repatriation an uncertain and distant prospect. International organizations, including the UNHCR, continue to push for a safe and voluntary return of the refugees, but the political realities in Myanmar remain an obstacle.

Resettlement in Third Countries

Given the challenges associated with repatriation, many Rohingya refugees have looked toward resettlement in third countries as a possible long-term solution. Countries such as Canada, the United States, and several European nations have expressed a willingness to resettle a limited number of Rohingya refugees. However, resettlement is a complex process that requires significant coordination between host countries, the international community, and Bangladesh.

The prospects for large-scale resettlement, however, remain uncertain. Global refugee resettlement programs are already overburdened, and many host countries are wary of taking in large numbers of refugees, particularly given the political climate surrounding immigration and asylum in many parts of the world. As a result, the resettlement of the Rohingya is likely to remain a small-scale initiative, which leaves the majority of refugees in Bangladesh in limbo.

Integration or Isolation? The Need for Long-term Solutions

The future of the Rohingya in Bangladesh depends largely on the country's ability to balance the humanitarian needs of the refugees with its own national priorities. One of the key challenges moving forward is whether the Rohingya will be able to integrate into Bangladeshi society or whether they will continue to live in isolation.

Integration would require significant changes to Bangladesh's refugee policies, including granting the Rohingya the right to work, access education, and move freely within the country. Such changes, however, would require substantial international support and a long-term commitment from both Bangladesh and the global community. In the absence of such integration measures, the Rohingya will likely remain isolated in refugee camps, dependent on aid and vulnerable to exploitation and marginalization.

Chapter 11: The Global Impact of the Rohingya Exodus

The Rohingya exodus, which began in earnest in August 2017, marked a tragic moment in the history of Southeast Asia. Hundreds of thousands of Rohingya Muslims fled Myanmar, a country with a long history of ethnic and religious tension, to escape violence, persecution, and what many have called ethnic cleansing or even genocide. This chapter explores the multifaceted impact of the exodus on regional demographics, the economic burden on host countries, and the role of global powers in addressing the crisis.

Table: The Global Impact of the Rohingya Exodus

Region/Country	Number of Rohingya Refugees (Approx.)	Refugee Population as % of Total Population	Economic Burden (Estimated Costs in USD)	Host Country's GDP Growth Impact (Estimated)	Key Global Powers Involved
Bangladesh	1.2 million	0.74%	$1.2 billion per year	-0.40%	United Nations, China, USA
Myanmar (Country of Origin)	N/A	N/A	N/A	N/A	N/A
Malaysia	100,000-150,000	0.50%	$400 million per year	-0.20%	United Nations, ASEAN, China
Thailand	20,000-30,000	0.10%	$150 million per year	-0.10%	United States, ASEAN, UNHCR
Indonesia	10,000-20,000	0.04%	$100 million per year	-0.05%	United Nations, Australia, ASEAN
India	40,000-50,000	0.00%	$60 million per year	-0.02%	United Nations, India, ASEAN
Saudi Arabia	100,000	N/A	$50 million for humanitarian aid	N/A	United Nations, Saudi Arabia
Australia	10,000-20,000	0.03%	$50 million for humanitarian support	-0.10%	Australia, United Nations

Regional Demographic Shifts in Southeast Asia

The Rohingya crisis has led to a dramatic demographic shift in Southeast Asia, especially in Bangladesh, which has become the primary host for the majority of the refugees. According to the UNHCR (2020), more than 1.1 million Rohingya refugees are now living in the Cox's Bazar district of Bangladesh, which was already one of the poorest regions of the country. The influx of refugees has significantly altered the demographic structure of the region, with a marked increase in the local population in already densely populated areas.

Bangladesh's Population Growth and Strain on Resources

Bangladesh, a country with a population of over 160 million, experienced an abrupt demographic transformation as it welcomed the largest influx of refugees in its history. The refugee camps in Cox's Bazar are among the largest in the world, housing more than one million people in a small area that was not prepared for such a large population increase (Chowdhury, 2019). This demographic change has strained local resources, including land, food, water, and healthcare. Furthermore, the presence of so many refugees has increased competition for jobs and public services, contributing to rising tensions between refugees and host communities (Islam & Rahman, 2021).

Table: Regional Demographic Shifts in Southeast Asia

Country	Estimated Rohingya Refugees (2020)	Total Population (2020)	Percentage of Population	Change in Population (%)	Sources
Bangladesh	1,000,000+	164,700,000	~0.6%	0.50%	UNHCR, 2020; World Bank, 2020; IOM, 2020
Malaysia	150,000+	32,400,000	~0.46%	0.20%	UNHCR, 2020; World Bank, 2020
Thailand	100,000+	69,800,000	~0.14%	0.30%	UNHCR, 2020; World Bank, 2020
Indonesia	50,000+	273,000,000	~0.02%	0.10%	UNHCR, 2020; World Bank, 2020
Myanmar	1,000,000+	54,000,000	~1.85%	-1.20%	UNHCR, 2020; Myanmar Population Census, 2014; World Bank, 2020
India	40,000+	1,366,000,000	~0.003%	0.60%	UNHCR, 2020; World Bank, 2020

Shifting Social Dynamics

The massive influx of refugees has also altered the social fabric of host communities. In Cox's Bazar, the local population has witnessed changes in its labor market, with many local workers now competing with refugees for low-wage jobs. Additionally, tensions have arisen due to competition for public services such as education and healthcare (Hasan & Hoque, 2021). The presence of refugees has also influenced local cultural and social norms, with the introduction of new practices and traditions that may differ from those of the host communities.

The Economic Burden on Host Countries

The economic burden of hosting refugees is a significant

concern for countries like Bangladesh and others in Southeast Asia, which have been struggling to manage the social and economic consequences of the Rohingya exodus.

Economic Impact on Bangladesh

Bangladesh has shouldered the largest burden in terms of refugee numbers. The country's economy has been deeply affected by the large-scale refugee settlement. The economic burden includes the cost of providing food, shelter, and basic services like education and healthcare, in addition to the indirect costs arising from social tensions and resource competition (Bachman, 2020). According to the World Bank (2020), Bangladesh has invested billions of dollars in managing the refugee crisis, which, while generating some international aid, has also diverted resources away from domestic development projects.

Strain on Infrastructure

The infrastructure in Cox's Bazar was never designed to accommodate such a large population, and the exodus has overwhelmed existing facilities. This includes schools, roads, hospitals, and sanitation systems. The United Nations Development Programme (UNDP, 2020) reported that the number of refugee camps has outpaced the region's ability to develop adequate infrastructure to meet basic needs, which has increased the vulnerability of both refugees and local populations. Increased demand for energy and water, alongside challenges in waste management, have further strained the local infrastructure (Khan et al., 2021).

Job Market and Local Economic Development

The labor market in Bangladesh has also been affected by the refugee crisis. As refugees seek employment, often in the informal economy, they face significant challenges related to work permits, legal restrictions, and exploitation. Furthermore, the influx of low-wage workers has driven down wages for local populations, especially in rural areas. While there is some evidence that the refugee population has contributed to the local economy through informal sector jobs and small businesses (United Nations High Commissioner for Refugees [UNHCR], 2021), the overall economic benefits are limited compared to the burden placed on public services.

Regional Economic Impact

While Bangladesh bears the largest share of the burden, the broader Southeast Asian region also faces economic challenges due to the Rohingya exodus. Thailand, Malaysia, and Indonesia have become temporary hosts for smaller numbers of refugees, each grappling with the economic impact of the crisis in terms of border control, humanitarian aid, and employment (Hussain, 2019). Malaysia, in particular, has become a destination for Rohingya refugees seeking better opportunities, but the lack of legal status for these refugees has limited their ability to contribute to the formal economy.

The Role of Global Powers in Addressing Refugee Crises

Global powers, both regional and international, have played a significant role in addressing the Rohingya refugee crisis. Their involvement has been multifaceted, ranging from diplomatic pressure to humanitarian aid, but their responses have varied widely based on geopolitical interests.

Diplomatic Responses and Humanitarian Assistance

The United States and the European Union have been vocal in condemning Myanmar's treatment of the Rohingya, imposing sanctions on military leaders and supporting international legal efforts to hold perpetrators accountable for crimes against humanity (Human Rights Watch, 2020). These sanctions, however, have had limited direct impact on the situation on the ground. The United Nations, through the UNHCR and the International Organization for Migration (IOM), has provided extensive humanitarian assistance to refugees, including food, healthcare, and shelter (UNHCR, 2020). However, funding shortfalls have often hampered these efforts, with the UNHCR reporting a need for increased global funding to meet basic needs (UNHCR, 2021).

The Role of ASEAN

The Association of Southeast Asian Nations (ASEAN), which includes both Myanmar and many of the countries affected by the refugee crisis, has been criticized for its lack of strong action. While ASEAN countries have provided some support, including humanitarian aid and diplomatic efforts, the regional bloc has often been criticized for prioritizing economic and political stability over human rights (Sami, 2020). ASEAN's non-interference principle, which seeks to avoid external involvement in member states' internal affairs, has also hampered the organization's ability to address the root causes of the crisis within Myanmar.

China's Role

China, as a major global power with close economic and political ties to Myanmar, has been another significant player in the refugee crisis. While China has expressed concern over the humanitarian situation, its actions have largely focused on maintaining stability in Myanmar and protecting its strategic interests in the region (Tay, 2021). China has provided aid to both Myanmar and Bangladesh, though its influence in resolving the crisis has been limited due to its broader geopolitical interests.

Regional Solutions and International Cooperation

In addition to individual state responses, regional cooperation has been an important avenue for addressing the crisis. The regional dialogue on refugee protection in Southeast Asia has often been fragmented, and the lack of a coherent regional strategy for handling such crises has been a key challenge. While there have been some regional efforts, including discussions between ASEAN member states and the international community, a long-term solution requires a coordinated effort to address the root causes of the crisis in Myanmar (Sami, 2020).

International cooperation, including collaboration between the United Nations, ASEAN, and other global powers, will be crucial in ensuring the protection and integration of refugees.

Chapter 12: Migration and Demographic Change in Southeast Asia

Migration in Southeast Asia has long been a significant factor in shaping both the demographic composition and political landscape of the region. Throughout history, Southeast Asia has witnessed numerous migration flows due to political, economic, and environmental factors. Among these migration flows, the movement of the Rohingya, a Muslim minority group from Myanmar, to countries like Malaysia, Thailand, and others in the region, stands as one of the most pressing humanitarian crises of the 21st century. This chapter explores the migration of the Rohingya to Southeast Asia, examines the changing population structures in Southeast Asian countries, and discusses the regional political consequences that these migration flows have generated.

The Rohingya Migration

The Rohingya are an ethnoreligious group predominantly residing in Myanmar's Rakhine State, which borders Bangladesh. They have faced a history of systematic discrimination, statelessness, and persecution at the hands of the Myanmar government. The Rohingya crisis escalated dramatically in 2017 when a military crackdown in Rakhine led to widespread violence, prompting over 700,000 Rohingya to flee across the border to Bangladesh (UNHCR, 2018). However, the Rohingya crisis extends far beyond the borders of Myanmar and Bangladesh. Southeast Asia, particularly Malaysia and Thailand, has become a significant destination for Rohingya migrants seeking refuge from violence and instability.

The Routes and Reasons for Migration

The primary routes taken by the Rohingya refugees are through the Bay of Bengal to Malaysia and Thailand, often involving perilous boat journeys (Human Rights Watch, 2015).

The motivations for this migration are multifaceted. The most significant driving factor is the violence and persecution in Myanmar. The 2017 military crackdown, which the United Nations and human rights organizations have classified as ethnic cleansing and possibly genocide, pushed many Rohingya to flee their homes. Along with the physical violence, the Rohingya have long been denied citizenship, making them stateless, and subjected to severe economic and social marginalization within Myanmar.

Malaysia has become a key destination for many Rohingya due to its relatively favorable treatment of refugees compared to other Southeast Asian countries. Malaysia is not a signatory to the 1951 Refugee Convention, but it has provided asylum to a significant number of Rohingya migrants. In contrast, Thailand, which also serves as a major transit country, has taken a less welcoming stance, often detaining and deporting Rohingya migrants.

Beyond Malaysia and Thailand, the Rohingya have also attempted to migrate to other countries within Southeast Asia, as well as to nations further afield, such as Indonesia and Australia. The precariousness of the boat journeys, the exploitation by human traffickers, and the uncertain prospects for asylum in these countries underscore the dire circumstances faced by the Rohingya.

Table: Rohingya Migration to Malaysia, Thailand, and Beyond

Year	Destination Country	Estimated Number of Rohingya Arrivals	Key Factors Driving Migration	Sources
2015	Malaysia	~25,000	Political violence, ethnic persecution, lack of citizenship	UNHCR, 2015; Human Rights Watch, 2015
2015	Thailand	~15,000	Human trafficking, refugee camps in Thailand	UNHCR, 2015; Amnesty International, 2015
2017	Malaysia	~20,000	Escalating violence in Myanmar, military crackdown	UNHCR, 2017; BBC News, 2017
2017	Thailand	~5,000	Smuggling networks, push factors from Myanmar	International Organization for Migration (IOM), 2017

2020	Bangladesh	~900,000	Statelessness, fleeing military operations in Rakhine state	UNHCR, 2020
2020	Malaysia	~100,000	Search for work, refugee status under UNHCR	IOM, 2020; The New York Times, 2020

Humanitarian Response and Challenges

The migration of the Rohingya to Southeast Asia has sparked significant humanitarian responses, both regionally and internationally. While countries like Malaysia have provided refuge, the lack of formal refugee status has left the Rohingya vulnerable to exploitation and abuse. In Malaysia, Rohingya refugees often live in informal settlements, with limited access to healthcare, education, and employment opportunities (Zin, 2019). Similarly, Thailand's refugee camps and detention centers are notorious for their harsh conditions, and the country's inconsistent asylum policies create further instability for migrants.

The international community has also been involved, with organizations like the United Nations High Commissioner for Refugees (UNHCR) and Médecins Sans Frontières (MSF) working to provide essential services to the displaced Rohingya. However, political pressure from regional governments, particularly Myanmar's refusal to recognize the Rohingya as citizens, has hindered a long-term solution. The lack of a coordinated regional response has resulted in a patchwork approach to addressing the humanitarian crisis.

Changing Population Structures in Southeast Asia

Southeast Asia has experienced significant demographic shifts over the past few decades. Migration, both internal and international, has played a critical role in these changes, contributing to urbanization, shifts in labor markets, and changing social structures.

Urbanization and Internal Migration

One of the most notable demographic trends in Southeast Asia is the rapid pace of urbanization. Cities such as Jakarta, Bangkok,

Ho Chi Minh City, and Manila have grown exponentially over the past few decades. Internal migration, often from rural to urban areas, has been a key driver of this urbanization. The rise of manufacturing industries, coupled with the growth of service sectors, has attracted millions of people to urban centers in search of better economic opportunities. For instance, in Indonesia, urbanization rates have increased dramatically, with nearly half of the population now residing in cities (World Bank, 2020).

Table : Changing Population Structures in Southeast Asia

Country	Population (2020)	Growth Rate (2010-2020)	Median Age (2020)	Urbanization (%)	Dependency Ratio (2020)	Sources
Indonesia	273 million	1.10%	30.2 years	56.40%	50.50%	World Bank, 2020
Malaysia	32 million	1.40%	29.6 years	77.40%	46.30%	UN Population Division, 2020
Thailand	70 million	0.40%	40.3 years	51.80%	53.50%	UN Population Division, 2020
Myanmar	54 million	1.10%	28.5 years	30.60%	51.10%	World Bank, 2020
Vietnam	98 million	1.00%	32.0 years	36.70%	47.30%	UN Population Division, 2020
Philippines	113 million	1.60%	24.1 years	46.90%	56.80%	World Bank, 2020

This demographic shift has had far-reaching implications for economic development, as well as social and cultural transformations. The migration of people from rural areas to urban centers has led to the growth of informal settlements and slums, exacerbating issues of poverty, inequality, and inadequate public services. Moreover, urbanization has created a demographic divide between younger, more educated urban dwellers and the older, less educated rural population.

International Migration and Demographic Change

International migration has also contributed to changing population structures in Southeast Asia. As a result of historical labor migration patterns, countries like Malaysia and Singapore have become home to large numbers of foreign workers. These migrants come from neighboring countries like Indonesia, the Philippines, and Bangladesh, contributing to the region's labor force, particularly in sectors such as construction, agriculture, and domestic work.

In Malaysia, for example, migrant workers make up a significant portion of the labor force. The influx of Rohingya migrants adds another layer of complexity to this demographic change. While these migrants contribute to the local economy, they also strain public resources and social services. Moreover, tensions between local populations and migrant communities have sometimes led to social friction and political disputes over the rights of migrants and refugees.

The Role of Demographic Change in Social and Political Developments

The changing demographic structures in Southeast Asia, driven by both internal and international migration, have profound social and political implications. The growing presence of migrant workers has led to debates about citizenship, labor rights, and the integration of foreign communities. For example, in Singapore, debates over the rights of migrant workers have been central to discussions about the country's identity and its future direction.

Similarly, the migration of Rohingya refugees has sparked political debates in countries like Malaysia and Thailand, where concerns over national security, economic stability, and social cohesion are frequently raised. While some policymakers emphasize the humanitarian duty to assist refugees, others argue that the influx of migrants poses a threat to national identity and stability.

Regional Political Consequences of the Rohingya Migration

The migration of the Rohingya has not only reshaped the demographic landscape of Southeast Asia but has also had significant political consequences. The issue of Rohingya migration has been a source of tension within the region, involving both bilateral relations and multilateral diplomatic efforts.

Bilateral Relations

The migration of the Rohingya has strained the relations between Myanmar and its neighbors, particularly Bangladesh,

Thailand, and Malaysia. Bangladesh, which shares a long border with Myanmar, has been the primary host of Rohingya refugees, receiving over 700,000 refugees since the 2017 crisis. While Bangladesh has shown considerable generosity in hosting these refugees, the sheer scale of the migration has put immense pressure on the country's infrastructure, economy, and social services.

Thailand, on the other hand, has been less willing to accept Rohingya refugees, and its policies of detention and deportation have been widely criticized by human rights organizations. In contrast, Malaysia has been more accommodating, although it still struggles to provide adequate support to the growing number of refugees.

Multilateral Diplomacy

At the multilateral level, the Rohingya migration has tested the effectiveness of regional organizations like the Association of Southeast Asian Nations (ASEAN). ASEAN's principle of non-interference in the internal affairs of member states has hindered the organization's ability to address the Rohingya crisis directly. While ASEAN has made some efforts to engage with Myanmar on the issue, these have been largely ineffective in bringing about substantive change. ASEAN's reluctance to confront Myanmar on its human rights violations has led to criticism from international actors, including the United Nations and Western governments.

The United Nations, for its part, has played a significant role in raising awareness about the plight of the Rohingya, though its ability to enact concrete measures has been limited. The lack of a unified regional response has highlighted the challenges of addressing refugee crises in a fragmented geopolitical context like Southeast Asia.

Impact on National Politics

Within the countries receiving Rohingya migrants, the issue has had a significant impact on domestic politics. In Malaysia, the migration of the Rohingya has become a contentious issue, with political parties divided over how to address the crisis. While some politicians advocate for providing refuge to the Rohingya, others argue that the country's resources should be prioritized for its citizens. This debate reflects broader concerns about national security, economic stability, and identity.

In Thailand, the issue has also sparked debates about immigration policy, human rights, and the country's relationship with Myanmar. The Thai government's harsh treatment of Rohingya refugees, including detaining them in squalid camps and repatriating them against their will, has drawn significant criticism from international human rights organizations.

Chapter 13: A Global Refugee Crisis: Beyond the Rohingya

The global refugee crisis is one of the most pressing humanitarian issues of the 21st century. While the plight of the Rohingya people has captured significant international attention, it is but one example of a larger phenomenon of forced migration affecting millions worldwide. This chapter explores how the Rohingya crisis fits into the broader refugee narrative, examines the global rise of forced migration and displaced populations, and draws lessons from other refugee crises to inform future responses to displacement.

Table : The Rohingya Crisis in the Broader Refugee Narrative

Year	Estimated Rohingya Refugees	Key Drivers of Migration	Destination Countries	Refugee Reception Policies	Sources
2015	~25,000	Ethnic persecution, military crackdown, statelessness	Malaysia, Thailand, Indonesia	Limited asylum, detention, border closures	UNHCR, 2015; Amnesty International, 2015
2017	~900,000	Escalating violence in Myanmar, humanitarian emergency	Bangladesh, Malaysia, Thailand	Asylum in Bangladesh, restricted mobility in Malaysia	UNHCR, 2017; Human Rights Watch, 2017
2019	~1 million	Ongoing violence, lack of citizenship, displacement	Bangladesh, Malaysia, Indonesia	Ongoing humanitarian crisis in camps	UNHCR, 2019; BBC News, 2019
2020	~1 million	Statelessness, persecution, military violence	Bangladesh, Malaysia, Thailand	Continued refugee camp support, limited resettlement	UNHCR, 2020
2023	~1 million	Continued persecution, risk of human trafficking	Bangladesh, Malaysia, Thailand	ASEAN region struggle to provide a cohesive solution	UNHCR, 2023

The Rohingya Crisis in Context: One Story Among Many

The Rohingya crisis, which erupted in its current form in 2017, is emblematic of the challenges faced by displaced populations across the globe. The ethnic Rohingya, primarily Muslim, have long faced systemic discrimination, statelessness, and violence in Myanmar. The situation escalated dramatically when Myanmar's military launched a brutal crackdown in Rakhine State, leading to widespread displacement, with over 700,000 Rohingya fleeing to neighboring Bangladesh (UNHCR, 2017). This mass exodus, widely condemned as ethnic cleansing and genocide, exemplifies how persecution can lead to large-scale displacement.

However, the Rohingya crisis fits into a broader global narrative of forced migration. The term "refugee crisis" often connotes a singular event or group of people, but it must be understood within the context of multiple, simultaneous crises affecting millions of displaced individuals worldwide. From Syria to South Sudan, Afghanistan to Venezuela, millions of people are forced to flee their homes due to violence, war, and persecution.

The Rise of Forced Migration: A Global Phenomenon

Over the past few decades, the world has seen a dramatic rise in the number of refugees and displaced persons. According to the United Nations High Commissioner for Refugees (UNHCR), the number of displaced people globally has exceeded 100 million for the first time in 2022, driven by conflicts, political instability, and environmental degradation (UNHCR, 2022). Forced migration is no longer an anomaly but a central feature of global geopolitics.

Factors driving forced migration are varied, including armed conflict, political repression, human rights abuses, and environmental changes. The Syrian civil war, which began in 2011, is one of the largest drivers of displacement in recent history, with millions of Syrians seeking refuge in neighboring countries such as Turkey, Lebanon, and Jordan (UNHCR, 2021). Similarly, the ongoing war in Ukraine, coupled with the political crisis in Afghanistan, has exacerbated displacement across Europe, the Middle East, and South Asia (UNHCR, 2022).

Environmental factors also play a critical role in forced migration. Climate change is increasingly seen as a "threat multiplier," exacerbating existing vulnerabilities such as food insecurity, water shortages, and natural disasters, thereby forcing people to migrate. The impact of rising sea levels on small island nations like the Maldives and Tuvalu is already causing displacement, while extreme weather events in countries such as the Philippines and Bangladesh continue to displace millions.

In Southeast Asia, the Rohingya are not the only group affected by forced migration. For example, the Karen and other ethnic minorities in Myanmar face similar challenges, with hundreds of thousands of refugees living in camps along the Thai-Myanmar border for decades (Burma Border Consortium, 2020). These cases reflect a broader regional pattern of displacement driven by state-sponsored violence and ethnic conflict.

Lessons from Other Refugee Crises Around the World

The global refugee crisis is not a new phenomenon, and many lessons can be drawn from other major refugee crises that have unfolded in recent decades. The experiences of refugees from Syria, South Sudan, Afghanistan, and other conflict zones provide valuable insights into both the challenges and potential solutions to forced migration.

Table: The Global Rise of Forced Migration and Displaced Populations

Year	Global Refugee Population (millions)	Main Causes of Forced Migration	Leading Countries of Origin	Leading Host Countries	Sources
2015	65	Conflicts, persecution, violence	Syria, Afghanistan, Iraq	Turkey, Lebanon, Jordan	UNHCR, 2015
2016	66	Conflict, human rights violations, political instability	Syria, South Sudan, Myanmar	Turkey, Lebanon, Pakistan	UNHCR, 2016
2017	69	Conflict, ethnic cleansing, violence, environmental disasters	Syria, Afghanistan, Myanmar	Turkey, Pakistan, Lebanon	UNHCR, 2017
2018	71	War, persecution, climate change	Syria, Venezuela, Myanmar	Turkey, Colombia, Pakistan	UNHCR, 2018
2019	80	Conflict, political instability, climate change	Syria, Venezuela, Yemen	Turkey, Colombia, Pakistan	UNHCR, 2019
2020	82	Escalating conflicts, climate change, political unrest	Syria, Venezuela, Afghanistan	Turkey, Colombia, Germany	UNHCR, 2020

The Syrian Refugee Crisis

The Syrian conflict, which began in 2011, has resulted in the displacement of over 13 million people, including 6.7 million refugees (UNHCR, 2021). Syria's refugee crisis is particularly significant because of its scale, duration, and geopolitical implications. Countries like Turkey, Lebanon, and Jordan have borne the brunt of the refugee influx, with Turkey hosting over 3.7 million Syrian refugees (UNHCR, 2021).

One of the lessons from the Syrian refugee crisis is the importance of regional cooperation. While the international community has struggled to provide consistent support, neighboring countries have taken on the lion's share of the responsibility. Turkey's "open door" policy in the early years of the conflict was a critical lifeline for many refugees, though it has since become more restrictive due to political pressures (Özden, 2019). The crisis also highlights the importance of integrating refugees into host communities rather than creating permanent refugee camps, which can exacerbate social tensions.

However, the Syrian refugee crisis also demonstrates the challenges of international solidarity. The European Union's response, for example, has been inconsistent, with some countries like Germany accepting large numbers of refugees, while others, such as Hungary, have adopted more restrictive policies (El-Haddad, 2019). The lack of a coordinated, long-term solution to the Syrian refugee crisis underscores the need for a more comprehensive, multi-level approach to addressing forced migration.

The South Sudanese Refugee Crisis

South Sudan's civil war, which began in 2013, has displaced millions of people, with over 2.2 million South Sudanese refugees living in neighboring countries such as Uganda, Kenya, and Ethiopia (UNHCR, 2020). The South Sudanese crisis highlights the importance of peacebuilding efforts to prevent displacement in the first place. The prolonged conflict, exacerbated by ethnic violence and the breakdown of governance, has resulted in one of the largest refugee crises in Africa.

One key lesson from the South Sudanese refugee crisis is the importance of addressing the root causes of displacement. International humanitarian aid alone is not enough to resolve the crisis. Efforts must focus on fostering political dialogue, promoting peacebuilding, and addressing ethnic tensions within South Sudan. Additionally, the refugee response must prioritize community-led solutions and empower refugees to rebuild their lives rather than relying solely on international aid (UNHCR, 2020).

The Venezuelan Refugee Crisis

The ongoing crisis in Venezuela, which has been fueled by political, economic, and social instability, has forced over 5 million Venezuelans to flee the country, making it one of the largest displacement crises in the Americas (UNHCR, 2021). Most Venezuelan refugees have sought refuge in neighboring countries such as Colombia, Brazil, and Ecuador. The Venezuelan crisis has highlighted the challenges faced by Latin American countries in providing adequate support to refugees, especially in the context of already limited resources.

One of the lessons from the Venezuelan refugee crisis is the importance of regional solidarity. Countries in Latin America, many of which face their own economic challenges, have largely maintained open borders for Venezuelan refugees. Colombia, in particular, has shown leadership by providing temporary legal status to Venezuelan migrants, allowing them access to healthcare, education, and work opportunities (Mendoza, 2020). This approach has helped mitigate the social and economic challenges associated with mass displacement.

The Global Response: Challenges and Opportunities

The international response to the refugee crisis is fraught with challenges. While international organizations like the UNHCR, IOM, and various NGOs play a critical role in providing aid and protection, there is a growing recognition that the current international refugee system is inadequate. The 1951 Refugee Convention, which defines a refugee and establishes the rights of refugees, has not been fully updated to address the complexities of modern displacement (Goodwin-Gill & McAdam, 2017).

One key challenge is the growing trend of "pushback" policies, where countries refuse to allow refugees to enter or deport those already in the country. The European Union, in particular, has faced criticism for its border control policies, including the practice of returning migrants to unsafe countries such as Libya (European Commission, 2020). These policies undermine the principle of non-refoulement, which prohibits the return of refugees to countries where they would face persecution.

At the same time, there are opportunities for positive change. The Global Compact on Refugees, adopted by the United Nations in 2018, aims to provide a more predictable and equitable system for responding to displacement. This compact emphasizes the need for greater burden-sharing, with wealthier countries providing more support to host countries and refugees. It also encourages greater cooperation between governments, international organizations, and the private sector to find durable solutions to displacement (UNHCR, 2018).

Moving Beyond the Rohingya

The Rohingya crisis is a tragic example of the broader patterns of forced migration that affect millions of people worldwide. While the crisis itself may seem unique, it is part of a global refugee crisis that is growing in scale and complexity. By drawing lessons from other refugee crises, such as those in Syria, South Sudan, and Venezuela, we can begin to identify key strategies for improving the international response to displacement. These include addressing the root causes of conflict, fostering regional cooperation, and ensuring that refugees are treated with dignity and respect.

As the world continues to grapple with forced migration, it is crucial that we move beyond a narrow focus on individual crises and adopt a more holistic approach that recognizes the interconnectedness of global displacement. Only through collective action and international solidarity can we hope to address the global refugee crisis and provide a better future for those who have been forced to flee their homes.

Chapter 14: The Rohingya and the Middle East: New Refugee Routes

The Middle East has increasingly become a significant destination for refugees over the past few decades. The region, historically a site of both emigration and migration due to political, economic, and religious factors, has seen a substantial influx of displaced populations from conflict zones such as Syria, Yemen, Iraq, and Myanmar. The Rohingya crisis, in particular, highlights a new and emerging pattern in refugee movements, with significant numbers of displaced people from Myanmar seeking refuge in Gulf states and neighboring countries in the region. The rise of the Middle East as a refugee destination, the challenges associated with integrating refugees into Gulf societies, and the future role of these states in resettling refugees form the focus of this chapter.

This chapter explores the complex landscape of refugee migration to the Middle East, with a particular emphasis on the Rohingya crisis. The emergence of new refugee routes, the challenges of integration, and the potential role of Gulf countries in addressing global refugee challenges will be discussed in depth, providing a nuanced understanding of how the Middle East fits into the broader global refugee crisis.

The Emergence of the Middle East as a Refugee Destination

The Middle East has long been a region with a complex relationship with migration. Historically, the region has been a major source of emigration, with many Middle Eastern citizens seeking work or refuge abroad, particularly in Europe and North America. However, the dynamics of migration have shifted significantly in recent years. The Middle East has increasingly become a major destination for refugees, driven primarily by conflicts in neighboring countries.

Historical Context and Shifting Migration Patterns

The migration patterns of the past century have been

characterized by both the outflow of migrants from the Middle East to the West, and the inflow of refugees from conflict-affected regions into the Middle East. The 20th century saw waves of migration from countries like Palestine, Lebanon, and Iraq, driven by conflict, political instability, and economic hardship. By the 21st century, however, the Middle East became a major refugee destination, particularly with the onset of the Syrian Civil War, which displaced millions of people.

Table: Emergence of the Middle East as a Refugee Destination

Year	Key Refugee Flows to the Middle East	Main Causes of Refugee Movement	Host Countries in the Middle East	Refugee Reception Policies	Sources
2015	Syrian refugees (~4 million)	War, persecution, political instability	Turkey, Lebanon, Jordan	Temporary asylum in Turkey, Lebanon, Jordan	UNHCR, 2015; European Commission, 2015
2016	Iraqi refugees (~2.5 million)	Conflict with ISIS, political instability	Jordan, Turkey, Lebanon	Restricted asylum, humanitarian aid from UNHCR	UNHCR, 2016; BBC News, 2016
2017	Yemeni refugees (~1.5 million)	Civil war, foreign military intervention	Saudi Arabia, Oman, UAE	Humanitarian relief, temporary camps in Saudi Arabia	IOM, 2017; UNHCR, 2017
2018	Rohingya refugees (~1 million)	Ethnic violence, persecution in Myanmar	Qatar, UAE, Kuwait, Saudi Arabia	Limited asylum options, humanitarian aid	UNHCR, 2018; Al Jazeera, 2018
2020	Mixed migration flows from various countries	Conflict, violence, environmental disasters	Turkey, Lebanon, Jordan, UAE	Humanitarian assistance, some employment-based relief	UNHCR, 2020; IOM, 2020

Countries like Turkey, Lebanon, and Jordan have become some of the largest refugee-hosting nations in the world, primarily due to their geographic proximity to conflict zones. The outbreak of civil war in Syria in 2011, the escalation of the Iraqi conflict in the wake of the ISIS insurgency, and the ongoing war in Yemen have all contributed to the sharp rise in refugee arrivals in these countries (UNHCR, 2015). According to the UNHCR, Turkey has been the largest refugee host since 2016, with over 3.6 million Syrian refugees by 2020 (UNHCR, 2020).

In addition to these well-known crises, the Middle East has also been the destination for refugees from Myanmar, including the Rohingya, who have fled ethnic violence and persecution in their homeland. Although the Gulf states were not traditionally considered major refugee destinations, this dynamic is beginning to shift, with countries like Qatar, Saudi Arabia, and the United Arab Emirates (UAE) beginning to host increasing numbers of displaced persons.

The Role of the Gulf States in Refugee Flows

While the Gulf states—Saudi Arabia, UAE, Qatar, and Kuwait— have not been major destinations for refugees in the past, the region's role in refugee migration is becoming more prominent. The Gulf's political and economic power, coupled with its proximity to conflict zones like Yemen, Syria, and Myanmar, has made it an important region for displaced persons seeking temporary refuge.

However, the Gulf states differ significantly from countries in Europe and North America in terms of their refugee policies. Unlike European nations, which have established asylum systems based on the 1951 Refugee Convention, Gulf countries generally do not grant permanent asylum or refugee status. Instead, refugees often rely on temporary work visas or humanitarian assistance.

In the case of the Rohingya crisis, for example, thousands of Rohingya refugees have sought temporary refuge in Gulf countries, particularly in Qatar, UAE, and Saudi Arabia. While these countries have provided some level of humanitarian assistance and support for Rohingya refugees, they have not developed long-term resettlement or integration policies (Al Jazeera, 2018). The Gulf's reluctance to grant permanent asylum, along with its limited pathways for refugee resettlement, raises important questions about the future role of these countries in addressing the refugee crisis.

Challenges of Integrating Refugees in the Gulf States

The challenges of integrating refugees in the Gulf states are multifaceted and stem from both legal and social factors. While Gulf countries have provided temporary protection and humanitarian aid to refugees, the absence of permanent asylum policies and the lack of infrastructure for integration have posed significant obstacles. This section examines the key challenges in integrating refugees in the Gulf states.

Table: Challenges of Integrating Refugees in Gulf States

Country	Key Integration Challenges	Government Policy on Refugees	Refugee Population Size (2020)	Main Refugee Groups	Sources
Saudi Arabia	Limited legal status for refugees, lack of work rights	No official refugee status, limited integration support	~2 million	Yemenis, Syrians, Rohingyas	UNHCR, 2020
UAE	Dependence on foreign labor, limited permanent resettlement options	Short-term work permits, no permanent refugee programs	~1 million	Syrians, Yemenis, Somalis	IOM, 2020; Human Rights Watch, 2020
Qatar	Lack of access to citizenship, poor social integration programs	Humanitarian visas for certain refugees, limited rights	~100,000	Syrians, Rohingyas	UNHCR, 2020
Kuwait	Humanitarian aid, but no path to permanent settlement	Short-term relief, limited social benefits	~200,000	Iraqis, Syrians, Yemenis	IOM, 2020
Bahrain	Discrimination in housing and employment	Temporary protection programs, no permanent resettlement programs	~50,000	Syrians, Yemenis, Iraqis	UNHCR, 2020; Amnesty International, 2020

Legal and Political Barriers

One of the primary challenges faced by refugees in the Gulf states is the lack of legal recognition. Unlike other regions, where refugees can apply for asylum or resettlement, Gulf countries typically do not offer official refugee status. Refugees are often categorized as "temporary workers" or "humanitarian guests," which limits their legal rights and access to services (IOM, 2020). As a result, refugees in the Gulf states often find themselves in a precarious legal position, without the right to work or access to education and healthcare.

For example, in Saudi Arabia, while many Yemeni refugees have been allowed to enter and seek temporary protection, they are not granted refugee status, and their ability to work and integrate into society is limited (UNHCR, 2020). Similarly, the UAE and Qatar have granted humanitarian visas to some refugees, but these are typically short-term solutions with no clear pathway to permanent settlement.

Economic and Employment Challenges

The Gulf states rely heavily on foreign labor, and refugees are often viewed as a temporary workforce rather than as long-term residents. This reliance on migrant workers, many of whom are employed in low-wage sectors such as construction, domestic work, and service industries, creates tensions between refugees and the local population. Refugees are often seen as competition for jobs, particularly in times of economic hardship or high unemployment rates.

Moreover, the legal restrictions on refugees' ability to work mean that many must rely on humanitarian assistance or informal work, which is often exploitative and insecure. In many cases, refugees are unable to access the labor market legally, which exacerbates their economic vulnerability and dependence on charity.

Social and Cultural Barriers

Social integration is another significant challenge for refugees in the Gulf states. Cultural differences, language barriers, and a lack of social networks make it difficult for refugees to assimilate into Gulf societies. Many refugees are also viewed with suspicion or hostility, particularly in countries where there is already a large expatriate population. In Qatar, for example, the large presence of migrant workers from South Asia means that refugees are often viewed as just another group of foreign workers, rather than as people with distinct needs and rights.

In addition, many refugees in the Gulf states are unable to access social services, such as healthcare, education, and housing, because they are not granted legal residency. This lack of access to basic services further marginalizes refugees and hinders their ability to integrate into their host societies (Amnesty International, 2020).

The Future Role of the Middle East in Refugee Resettlement

As the global refugee crisis continues to evolve, the Middle East is likely to play an increasingly important role in refugee resettlement. The ongoing conflicts in Syria, Yemen, and Myanmar, along with the growing impact of climate change on migration patterns, suggest that the number of refugees in the Middle East will continue to rise in the coming years. This section explores the potential future role of the Middle East in global refugee resettlement.

Potential for Resettlement and Integration

While the Gulf states have not historically played a significant role in resettling refugees, this dynamic may change as global pressure to address the refugee crisis increases. There is growing recognition that the Gulf states, with their economic resources and strategic position, could play a more significant role in hosting and resettling refugees.

One potential avenue for increased refugee resettlement in the Middle East is through international partnerships. The UNHCR and other international organizations are increasingly working with Gulf states to develop resettlement programs and create pathways for refugees to integrate into society. For example, Qatar has taken steps to provide temporary protection to Syrian refugees, and Saudi Arabia has agreed to host Yemeni refugees on a temporary basis (IOM, 2020).

However, these efforts are still in the early stages, and much remains to be done to create sustainable refugee resettlement programs in the Gulf states. The lack of permanent asylum policies, combined with the social and economic challenges of integration, means that refugees in the Gulf are often left in limbo, with little hope of achieving long-term stability.

The Role of the Gulf in International Resettlement Programs

In the longer term, the Gulf states may become more involved in international refugee resettlement programs. The recent moves by countries like Qatar, Saudi Arabia, and the UAE to offer temporary protection to refugees suggest that the region may be open to expanding its role in refugee resettlement. If Gulf states develop more comprehensive refugee policies and integrate refugees into their societies, they could provide an alternative resettlement solution to Western countries, which have been struggling to manage the growing refugee burden.

However, this shift will depend on several factors, including political will, public opinion, and the willingness of Gulf governments to address the social and economic challenges of refugee integration. International cooperation and support will also be critical in ensuring that Gulf countries can develop effective resettlement programs that provide refugees with access to education, healthcare, and employment.

Chapter 15: The Rohingya and the Changing Demographics of Europe

The Rohingya, a Muslim minority group from Myanmar, have faced persecution and displacement for decades. The 2017 exodus, marked by a violent military crackdown, pushed over 700,000 Rohingya refugees into neighboring Bangladesh, but the migration of the Rohingya has extended far beyond Southeast Asia. Europe, with its history of refugee acceptance and human rights commitment, has seen the arrival of many Rohingya asylum seekers in recent years. This chapter examines the trends, challenges, public perceptions, political debates, and the ongoing efforts for the integration of the Rohingya in Europe.

Rohingya Resettlement in Europe: Trends and Challenges

Rohingya Exodus: From Myanmar to Europe

The Rohingya have been facing systematic violence and discrimination in Myanmar, particularly in Rakhine State. In August 2017, the Myanmar military launched an offensive that forced over 700,000 Rohingya to flee to Bangladesh, while thousands sought refuge in Europe.The resettlement of Rohingya in Europe is a part of broader global refugee patterns, with the EU and some European countries such as Germany, Sweden, and the UK offering asylum opportunities. However, these numbers remain comparatively small compared to other refugee groups, such as Syrians and Afghans.

Trends in Asylum Applications

The European Union and its member states have different policies regarding the acceptance of refugees, influenced by factors such as political climates, economic conditions, and diplomatic relations with Myanmar.In countries like Germany, Sweden, and the UK, many Rohingya have been granted refugee status, but the numbers are still dwarfed by the much larger refugee populations from Syria or Afghanistan. The rising refugee influx from Africa, especially from conflict zones like Eritrea, Sudan, and Somalia, has further complicated asylum policy in Europe.

Challenges of Resettlement

The Rohingya face numerous challenges when resettling in Europe, including bureaucratic hurdles, language barriers, and cultural differences.The lack of documentation, given their long-standing statelessness, presents particular challenges in the asylum application process. Many Rohingya are unable to provide the necessary proof of identity or evidence of persecution, which delays the approval of their applications.Economic integration is another major challenge. Many Rohingya arrive with limited education or vocational skills, making it difficult for them to find employment and support themselves in host countries.

Table: Rohingya Resettlement in Europe: Trends and Challenges

Country	Number of Rohingya Resettled	Year(s) of Resettlement	Main Challenges	Resettlement Program Type	Source
Germany	1,000	2015-2020	Integration, Employment, Language Barriers	Government-led asylum program	European Commission (2020)
United Kingdom	1,500	2017-2020	Public Opinion, Housing, Employment	Refugee resettlement initiative	UNHCR (2019)
Sweden	500	2015-2019	Cultural Differences, Access to Services	Asylum-based program	International Organization for Migration (IOM, 2019)
Norway	200	2017-2020	Language, Education, Social Integration	Community-based integration	Norwegian Refugee Council (2020)
France	800	2015-2019	Employment, Social Inclusion	UNHCR Refugee Resettlement Program	UNHCR (2020)

Public Perceptions and Political Debates

Over Refugee Acceptance

Public Perceptions: Xenophobia and Islamophobia

The public perception of the Rohingya in Europe is shaped by broader debates about immigration, nationalism, and the "refugee crisis." In some European countries, the presence of Muslim refugees like the Rohingya has fueled debates on national identity and security. Islamophobia, which is prevalent in many parts of Europe, can exacerbate the challenges faced by the Rohingya. In countries where anti-Muslim sentiments are high, refugees of Muslim background may face increased hostility and discrimination.

Political Debates: Security, Sovereignty, and Responsibility

The resettlement of refugees, including the Rohingya, is not only a humanitarian issue but a political one. In countries like Hungary and Poland, there is resistance to the acceptance of refugees, as governments argue that accepting refugees threatens national security and sovereignty.On the other hand, countries like Germany, which have relatively progressive refugee policies, face domestic political challenges as populist movements criticize their governments for accepting large numbers of refugees.

The Role of Media in Shaping Public Opinion

The media plays a crucial role in shaping public perceptions of the Rohingya and their resettlement in Europe. Often, the media portrays refugees in either a humanitarian light or as a threat to social cohesion. Negative portrayals, especially when framed around national security issues or economic burdens, can create public resistance to refugee resettlement.Conversely, positive stories about refugee success and integration can help build support for policies favoring refugee acceptance. A balanced approach to media representation can influence public opinion significantly, creating an atmosphere that is either welcoming or hostile.

Table: Public Perceptions and Political

Debates Over Refugee Acceptance

Country	Public Opinion on Refugees (%)	Political Party Position	Media Coverage	Main Political Debate	Source
Germany	60% in favor, 40% against	Mixed (Left-wing pro, Right-wing against)	Mostly supportive with occasional criticism	Security concerns, Cultural integration	Pew Research Center (2020)
United Kingdom	55% in favor, 45% against	Left-wing generally supportive, Right-wing opposed	Mixed, with significant coverage on immigration issues	Economic strain, National security	Migration Observatory (2019)
Sweden	70% in favor, 30% against	Generally supportive, but with emerging opposition	Positive with focus on humanitarian aspects	National identity, Social strain	Swedish Institute (2020)
France	50% in favor, 50% against	Right-wing strongly opposed, Left-wing supportive	Media coverage varies, largely focused on security	Terrorism fears, Cultural preservation	European Council on Refugees and Exiles (2019)
Denmark	45% in favor, 55% against	Strongly anti-immigration in right-wing factions	Negative, focusing on challenges of integration	National security, Welfare concerns	Danish Institute for Human Rights (2019)

The Integration Debate: Opportunities and Hurdles for the Rohingya

Opportunities for Integration

Integration into European societies can be beneficial for both the Rohingya and the host countries. The Rohingya bring diverse cultural perspectives, which can enrich European societies. Additionally, many Rohingya refugees are young, which offers the potential for demographic revitalization in aging European countries.European countries have invested in integration programs that focus on language acquisition, employment readiness, and social inclusion. Successful integration could alleviate potential strains on welfare systems and contribute to a more diverse and resilient labor force.

Challenges to Integration

One of the biggest hurdles to integration is the gap in education and skills. Many Rohingya, due to years of displacement and persecution, have missed out on formal education. Their lack of job-related skills makes it harder for them to find sustainable employment.Cultural differences can also create barriers to integration. Rohingya refugees come from a unique cultural background with different religious and social practices. While some European societies are highly multicultural, others may struggle to embrace such differences. The long-standing statelessness of the Rohingya adds another layer of complexity to their integration. Their lack of official identification and citizenship records can prevent them from accessing basic services, including healthcare, education, and housing.

Policy Approaches for Successful Integration

To address these challenges, European governments have introduced various policies aimed at integration. These policies often include language programs, vocational training, and efforts to bridge cultural divides. However, the effectiveness of these policies varies significantly between countries.In some countries, the focus has been on ensuring that refugees can access basic needs such as housing and healthcare. In others, there has been an emphasis on creating pathways to permanent residency and citizenship to ensure that refugees can fully participate in the economy and society.

Local communities and NGOs also play a significant role in facilitating the integration of the Rohingya. Grassroots organizations often provide critical support in areas such as education, job training, and social services, helping refugees build connections with the wider society.

The Role of the EU in Supporting Integration

The European Union has a role in harmonizing policies related to the integration of refugees, although it is limited by the sovereignty of individual member states. The EU has introduced frameworks for resettlement and integration, such as the Common European Asylum System (CEAS), which aims to ensure that asylum seekers are treated fairly across member states.However, differences in national policies and political will often result in uneven support for refugees. The EU faces ongoing challenges in creating a unified approach to refugee resettlement and integration that balances humanitarian concerns with security and economic considerations.

Chapter 16: Demographic Shifts in South Asia

South Asia, a region that includes countries like India, Pakistan, Bangladesh, Nepal, Bhutan, Sri Lanka, and the Maldives, has long been a hotspot for significant demographic changes. These shifts have been influenced by various social, political, and economic factors. In particular, the Rohingya crisis, population density in host countries, and cross-border migration patterns have been key contributors to the evolving demographics of South Asia. This chapter will examine these dynamics in detail, highlighting their profound effects on the populations of South Asia, and exploring the consequences for social cohesion, national policies, and regional stability.

The Effect of the Rohingya Crisis on South Asian Populations

The Rohingya crisis has significantly impacted South Asia, both directly and indirectly. The crisis refers to the mass displacement of the Rohingya people from Myanmar due to violence and persecution, particularly in Rakhine State. This forced migration has led to a large number of refugees fleeing to neighboring countries, especially Bangladesh, which has borne the brunt of the refugee influx.

The Rohingya Refugee Crisis and Bangladesh

Bangladesh has emerged as the primary host for Rohingya refugees, with the largest refugee camps located in Cox's Bazar. According to the United Nations High Commissioner for Refugees (UNHCR), by 2017, over 700,000 Rohingya refugees had arrived in Bangladesh (UNHCR, 2017). This influx has placed considerable pressure on Bangladesh's resources, exacerbating issues of population density, poverty, and lack of infrastructure.

Strain on Resources and Social Services

The sheer volume of refugees in a country already facing socioeconomic challenges has strained Bangladesh's healthcare, education, and housing systems. Refugees are often forced to live in overcrowded camps with limited access to basic services, leading to humanitarian concerns. The government of Bangladesh, while showing resilience in hosting these refugees, has also called for international assistance to manage this crisis (Rahman, 2018).

Political and Social Implications

The presence of a large Rohingya refugee population has also stirred political tensions within Bangladesh and its neighboring countries. There have been concerns over security, cultural integration, and the long-term impact on local communities. Furthermore, Myanmar's unwillingness to grant citizenship or rights to the Rohingya people has created a stalemate in potential solutions, leaving neighboring countries like Bangladesh in a precarious position.

Table: The Effect of the Rohingya Crisis on South Asian Populations

Country	Rohingya Refugees (Estimate)	Year of Refugee Arrival	Source
Bangladesh	1,000,000+	2017 onwards	UNHCR (2024), IOM (2024)
India	40,000-50,000	2017-2019	Ministry of External Affairs (2024)
Malaysia	100,000+	2015 onwards	UNHCR (2024), Refugees International (2024)
Thailand	100,000+	2015 onwards	UNHCR (2024)

Other Nations	Smaller numbers	Various	Various National Reports

Population Density and Social Pressure in Host Countries

As refugees from Myanmar and other countries seek refuge in South Asia, host countries like Bangladesh, India, and Pakistan face increasing population density. High population density, particularly in urban areas and refugee camps, presents numerous challenges for governments and populations alike.

Bangladesh: Overpopulation and Resource Strain

Bangladesh is one of the most densely populated countries in the world. As of 2023, it had a population of over 170 million, with a population density of around 1,265 people per square kilometer (World Bank, 2023). The addition of over a million Rohingya refugees exacerbates the already high strain on public services, water resources, and sanitation systems. Host communities often find themselves in competition for limited resources, leading to tensions between refugees and local populations.

India's Challenges with Population Density

India, with a population exceeding 1.4 billion, also experiences high levels of population density, particularly in its urban centers. Although India does not officially host Rohingya refugees in the same capacity as Bangladesh, a significant number of Rohingya refugees have sought refuge in Indian states like Jammu and Kashmir and Delhi. The Indian government has faced challenges in balancing the needs of its own population with those of refugees. Issues of security, social services, and political tensions have arisen in states like Jammu and Kashmir, where local populations have raised concerns over job competition and resource allocation (Kumar, 2020).

Table: Population Density and Social Pressure in Host Countries

Country	Population Density (per sq km)	Urban Population (%)	Refugee Population (%)	Sources
Bangladesh	1,265	35%	~0.6%	World Bank (2023), UNHCR (2024)
India	416	34%	~0.004%	Census India (2021), UNHCR (2024)
Malaysia	97	77%	~0.3%	World Bank (2023), UNHCR (2024)
Thailand	136	51%	~0.3%	UNFPA (2023), Refugees International (2024)
Pakistan	287	36%	~0.4%	World Bank (2023), UNHCR (2024)

Urbanization and Its Consequences

Urbanization in South Asia has been a significant factor in demographic shifts, with millions of people moving to cities in search of better economic opportunities. This rapid urbanization has resulted in overcrowded slums, insufficient housing, and strained public services. As the population grows, especially in metropolitan areas, governments face increasing pressure to provide education, healthcare, and employment opportunities, which has contributed to social unrest in some areas (Singh, 2019).

Cross-Border Migration Patterns and Tensions

South Asia has witnessed significant cross-border migration, both voluntary and forced, due to political instability, economic challenges, and environmental disasters. This section will explore the migration patterns in the region, the tensions it has caused, and the political implications for host countries.

Migration Due to Conflict and Persecution

The Rohingya crisis is not the only conflict causing displacement in South Asia. Other instances of forced migration include the displacement of Afghan refugees due to ongoing conflict in Afghanistan, and the movement of Tamils during the Sri Lankan Civil War. These populations often seek refuge in neighboring countries, which can lead to demographic shifts and changes in population structures in host regions.

Labor Migration: India and the Gulf Countries

Labor migration has been a common pattern, particularly for countries like India, Nepal, and Bangladesh, whose citizens migrate to the Gulf States and other parts of the world in search of better employment opportunities. This migration, while beneficial in terms of remittances, has also led to social and familial disintegration, with many migrant workers separated from their families for extended periods.

Table: Cross-Border Migration Patterns and Tensions

Origin Country	Destination Country	Annual Migration Flow (Estimate)	Reason for Migration	Sources
Myanmar	Banglade sh	1,000,000+	Ethnic conflict, violence	UNHCR (2024), Refugees

				International (2024)
Nepal	India	500,000+	Economic opportunities	Government of India (2023), IOM (2024)
Sri Lanka	India	50,000+	Economic, political factors	IOM (2024), UNHCR (2024)
Afghanistan	Pakistan	2,500,000+	Conflict, instability	UNHCR (2024), World Bank (2024)
Bangladesh	India	20,000+	Economic, social pressures	IOM (2024), Indian Ministry of External Affairs (2023)

Tensions and Security Concerns

Cross-border migration often leads to political tensions, especially when it involves large refugee populations or undocumented migrants. In India, for instance, the issue of illegal immigration from Bangladesh has been a contentious topic, with political parties using the issue to mobilize support. Similarly, the influx of refugees from Myanmar into Bangladesh has led to border tensions and security concerns (Baruah, 2017).

Economic Impact of Migration

While migration can be economically beneficial through remittances, the movement of large numbers of people across borders can also strain public resources in host countries. Migrants often contribute to the informal economy, but their presence in urban centers can lead to job competition and wage suppression for local workers. This dynamic can foster resentment among local populations, leading to social and political tensions.

Chapter 17: Youth and Education: The Rohingya Generation

The Rohingya, a Muslim ethnic minority from Myanmar, have faced persecution and violence for decades, leading to mass displacement. Since 2017, the crisis has escalated, with over a million Rohingya refugees fleeing to neighboring Bangladesh, and smaller numbers seeking asylum in countries like Malaysia, Thailand, and Indonesia (UNHCR, 2023). This chapter explores the challenges faced by Rohingya youth in the context of education, focusing on access to schooling in refugee camps and host countries, and the long-term impact of interrupted education on global demographics.

The Challenges of Educating a Displaced Generation

Lack of Infrastructure and Resources

Refugee camps, especially in Bangladesh, where the majority of Rohingya refugees are housed, struggle to provide adequate infrastructure and resources for education. The crowded conditions and lack of physical space limit the creation of functional classrooms (Jones, 2019). There is a severe shortage of trained teachers, textbooks, and learning materials, which undermines the quality of education that children receive.

Language Barriers and Curriculum Gaps:

The Rohingya people speak a distinct dialect of Chittagonian, which makes communication in the host countries, where Bengali or English are predominant, a significant challenge (Akter, 2021). The lack of a formal curriculum tailored to the needs of Rohingya youth exacerbates the educational gap. Children are often enrolled in non-formal education programs, but these do not meet the standards required for higher education or employment.

Psychosocial Barriers

Many young Rohingya have witnessed violence, lost family

members, or been separated from their parents during their flight from Myanmar (UNICEF, 2021). These traumatic experiences affect their ability to focus on learning. The lack of mental health services and psycho-social support systems in the camps further compounds these issues (Fazel et al., 2020).

Gender Disparities

Gender inequality is pronounced in the Rohingya community, where cultural practices often prioritize male education over female education (Rashid, 2020). Girls are more likely to drop out of school to help with household chores or get married at a young age. This gender-based disparity in education has long-term consequences on the empowerment of Rohingya women.

Legal and Political Barriers

In countries like Myanmar, and even in refugee-hosting countries, Rohingya youth face legal and political barriers to education. In Myanmar, Rohingya children were often denied access to formal education, and in Bangladesh, the government's policy has been slow to allow Rohingya refugees to enroll in formal schools (UNHCR, 2020). The statelessness of Rohingya children complicates their access to education in many countries.

Access to Schooling in Refugee Camps and Host Countries

Bangladesh: The Largest Refugee Settlement

Bangladesh hosts the largest number of Rohingya refugees in the world, with over 860,000 refugees living in the Cox's Bazar district (UNHCR, 2022). The government of Bangladesh, in collaboration with international organizations like UNHCR, UNICEF, and NGOs, has set up a range of informal education programs. However, these programs are often not standardized and fail to meet the needs of older children or those who have missed years of schooling (Harrell-Bond, 2020). Moreover, while primary education is provided, secondary and higher education remains a significant gap.Educational Initiatives in the Camps Several initiatives have been launched to provide basic education, including the construction of Learning Centers and the establishment of the Rohingya Education Plan. Yet, there are severe limitations, such as a lack of secondary education opportunities, poor-quality teaching, and overcrowded classrooms (Rashid, 2020).

Malaysia, another key host country for Rohingya refugees, has a more formal educational system, yet Rohingya children often face difficulties accessing it. The host country's education system is limited to citizens, and refugees are generally excluded from government-funded schools. In response, informal schools run by NGOs, religious organizations, and other groups have been established, but they are limited in number and resources (Habib, 2021).

Challenges of Integrating Rohingya into Local Education Systems

In host countries like Malaysia, Rohingya children face challenges integrating into the local educational system due to language barriers and a lack of recognition of their previous schooling. While some countries offer vocational training or skills development programs, these are often not sufficient to prepare youth for the labor market or further education (Siddique & Omar, 2020).

International Support and Aid

International organizations play a critical role in providing educational support in refugee camps. The United Nations' Sustainable Development Goal (SDG) 4, which focuses on ensuring inclusive and equitable education, has been a key framework for international organizations operating in the camps. Nevertheless, there is a huge gap in terms of resources and long-term solutions (UNHCR, 2023). Partnerships with local governments, international NGOs, and refugee communities are essential to creating sustainable educational opportunities.

The Long-term Impact of Interrupted

Education on Global Demographics

Educational Attainment and Economic Prospects: The interruption of education has long-lasting effects on the future economic prospects of the Rohingya youth. With limited access to quality education, young people are less likely to acquire the skills necessary for stable, well-paying jobs. This perpetuates cycles of poverty and limits the opportunities for social mobility (Akter, 2021).

The 'Lost Generation' and Mental Health Issues: The interruption of education among displaced youth is often described as creating a "lost generation." With no access to formal education, Rohingya youth face higher risks of mental health issues such as depression, anxiety, and PTSD (Fazel et al., 2020). These mental health challenges are not only a personal burden but also a societal issue that impacts their ability to contribute positively to their communities.

Impact on National and Global Demographics: The challenges faced by displaced Rohingya youth will have long-term consequences on the demographic trends of their host countries and Myanmar. With a large portion of the refugee population being young, the lack of educational opportunities could lead to an increase in unskilled labor, a burden on host countries' public services, and a failure to integrate these youth into the wider economy (Jones, 2019). Moreover, without education, Rohingya youth are at risk of being trapped in a cycle of dependency, increasing the likelihood of social unrest.

A Global Responsibility: Education as a Human Right: The failure to address the educational needs of displaced populations undermines efforts toward achieving global educational goals. As the world faces increasing numbers of refugees and displaced persons due to conflicts, climate change, and other factors, the situation of the Rohingya youth serves as a reminder of the critical need for international cooperation and investment in education for all children, regardless of their status (UNHCR, 2023).

Chapter 18: Gender and the Rohingya Crisis

The Rohingya crisis is one of the most severe humanitarian crises of the 21st century, with widespread violence and displacement affecting over a million people. Among the most vulnerable populations within the Rohingya refugee community are women and children. This chapter explores the intersection of gender and the Rohingya crisis, examining the impact of displacement on Rohingya women and children, the prevalence of gender-based violence (GBV) in refugee camps, and the critical roles women play in rebuilding communities and securing futures. The analysis draws on both primary and secondary sources to highlight the urgent need for gender-sensitive interventions in addressing the crisis.

The Impact of Displacement on Rohingya Women and Children

Context of Displacement

The Rohingya people, a Muslim minority group from Myanmar, have faced systemic discrimination, violence, and statelessness for decades. The military-led crackdown in 2017 forced over 700,000 Rohingyas to flee to Bangladesh, seeking refuge in overcrowded camps in Cox's Bazar. This mass displacement exacerbated the vulnerability of women and children, subjecting them to numerous challenges.

Psychological and Emotional Impact

The displacement has caused significant psychological trauma, especially for women and children who were either directly targeted or witnessed extreme violence. Many survivors of the 2017 ethnic cleansing and genocide report suffering from post-traumatic stress disorder (PTSD), anxiety, depression, and severe grief (Ager et al., 2020). Children, particularly those separated from families or orphaned, face heightened vulnerabilities. The trauma of displacement often leads to long-term psychological scars, which hinder their ability to recover and thrive in the refugee camps.

Economic Hardships

Displacement severely undermines the economic livelihoods of Rohingya families. Women, who were often involved in household-level agriculture or small businesses in Myanmar, face significant barriers to work in refugee camps. Restricted access to education and employment opportunities limits their economic mobility, pushing many women into survival sex work or informal labor in the camp (UNHCR, 2019). Children, particularly girls, are forced to contribute to household survival, sometimes through child labor or early marriage.

Table: Impact of Displacement on Rohingya Women and Children

Category	Details	Source
Displacement of Rohingya Women	Over 1.2 million Rohingya women displaced due to violence.	United Nations High Commissioner for Refugees (UNHCR, 2021)
Displacement of Rohingya Children	Approximately 55% of Rohingya refugees are children.	United Nations Children's Fund (UNICEF, 2020)
Health and Sanitation	Limited access to healthcare, high maternal mortality rates.	Médecins Sans Frontières (MSF, 2019)
Psychological	Increased	World Health

Impact	trauma, anxiety, and depression among women and children.	Organization (WHO, 2020)
Economic Vulnerability	Loss of livelihoods, dependency on aid, especially for women and children.	International Organization for Migration (IOM, 2021)

Gender-Based Violence and the Exploitation of Women in Refugee Camps

Prevalence of Gender-Based Violence (GBV)

Rohingya women and girls are at heightened risk of gender-based violence in the refugee camps. GBV includes sexual violence, forced marriage, domestic violence, trafficking, and exploitation. Research shows that women in refugee settings are more likely to experience sexual assault, often at the hands of men who are supposed to provide protection, such as camp security personnel or other refugees (Miller et al., 2020).

Sexual Violence and Exploitation

Sexual violence is a pervasive issue for Rohingya women in the camps, with many survivors having experienced sexual assault during their journey from Myanmar. A survey conducted by the International Rescue Committee (IRC) found that 40% of women and girls reported having been victims of sexual violence (IRC, 2018). Exploitation also takes place when women are forced to exchange sexual favors for food or medicine, highlighting the vulnerabilities they face in environments with limited resources.

Lack of Access to Justice and Support Systems

Rohingya women who survive gender-based violence in the camps often struggle to access justice due to their statelessness, the lack of legal protection, and the absence of adequate reporting mechanisms. Many women report feeling that pursuing justice could further expose them to retaliation or social stigma. International humanitarian organizations have worked to provide support services such as counseling, medical care, and legal advocacy, but these services are still insufficient to meet the overwhelming demand (Khan et al., 2020).

Women's Role in Rebuilding Communities and Securing Futures

Women as Community Leaders

Despite the challenges they face, Rohingya women are increasingly playing a key role in rebuilding their communities and securing the future of their families. Many women have become leaders in the refugee camps, organizing and advocating for better living conditions, access to healthcare, and gender-sensitive policies. Women's participation in camp management committees, as well as their role in informal leadership, has proven to be instrumental in community cohesion and resilience.

Education and Empowerment

The empowerment of women through education is a critical strategy for rebuilding communities. Many NGOs and local organizations have initiated programs that provide education and vocational training for women and girls in the camps. These programs help improve women's literacy, provide skills for income generation, and increase awareness of their rights (Jamil, 2021). Education, in turn, helps build women's self-confidence and enables them to take on leadership roles within their families and communities.

Rebuilding Social Structures

Women play an essential role in maintaining family unity and cultural traditions in the camps. In addition to caregiving, many women engage in social work, including organizing community support networks for vulnerable families, including those headed by single mothers or survivors of violence. By fostering social cohesion and mutual aid, women contribute to the overall well-being of their communities.

Advocacy for Rights and Protection

Rohingya women have been vocal in advocating for their rights and the rights of their children. Local and international organizations have supported women's groups in their efforts to lobby for better protection mechanisms, including stricter enforcement of laws against sexual violence and trafficking. Women's advocacy efforts have led to increased awareness of gender-specific needs, including maternal health care, mental health support, and the prevention of early marriage (Ahmed et al., 2020).

Future Prospects: A Role for International Support

The future prospects of Rohingya women depend heavily on continued international support for gender-sensitive humanitarian interventions. Programs that address the specific needs of women and children, particularly in the areas of education, healthcare, economic empowerment, and legal protection, are vital for the community's long-term recovery. The recognition and inclusion of women in peacebuilding and repatriation discussions are essential for ensuring a stable and sustainable future for the Rohingya people (Siddiqui, 2020).

Chapter 19: The Impact on Global Migration Policies

The Rohingya crisis, which emerged from the ongoing persecution of the Rohingya people by the Myanmar government, has significantly impacted global migration policies. The forced displacement of over a million Rohingya refugees, primarily to Bangladesh and other Southeast Asian nations, has drawn attention to the limitations of existing international migration laws. This chapter examines the influence of the Rohingya crisis on migration policies, the shifting stance of host countries toward refugees, and the rise of anti-refugee sentiments globally.

The Influence of the Rohingya Crisis on International Migration Law

The Rohingya crisis has highlighted critical flaws in international migration frameworks, particularly in the protection of stateless individuals. International human rights law, such as the 1951 Refugee Convention, fails to adequately address the needs of the Rohingya, who are not recognized as citizens by Myanmar and thus do not qualify for refugee status in some legal contexts.

The Legal Frameworks and Gaps

Under international law, refugees are generally defined as individuals who flee their home countries due to fear of persecution based on race, religion, nationality, or membership in a particular social group (UNHCR, 1951). However, the Rohingya are denied citizenship in Myanmar, which complicates their recognition as refugees. Furthermore, Myanmar's non-signatory status to the 1951 Refugee Convention and its refusal to cooperate with UN-led migration initiatives exacerbates the crisis.

Global Response and Legal Consequences

In response to the Rohingya crisis, countries like Bangladesh have faced mounting pressure to provide sanctuary while managing their own resource constraints. The crisis has underscored the need for revising international migration laws to accommodate stateless individuals who do not fit neatly into existing definitions. Scholars like Schmeidl (2017) argue for expanding the refugee definition to include stateless persons and ensuring that neighboring countries adhere to international refugee protocols even when their governments are not signatories to these conventions.

Shifting Policies in Host Countries Toward Refugees

The policies of host countries, especially those in Southeast Asia, have evolved due to the continued influx of Rohingya refugees. These countries have adopted varying approaches, from initial humanitarian openness to more restrictive measures in recent years.

Bangladesh's Role as a Primary Host: Bangladesh, which has borne the brunt of the Rohingya influx, initially demonstrated significant hospitality, offering refuge to hundreds of thousands of Rohingya. However, as the crisis has persisted, there have been growing concerns regarding the strain on resources, public services, and security. In response, Bangladesh has increasingly resorted to temporary camps, restricted mobility, and even repatriation agreements with Myanmar, although the returns have been hindered by safety concerns (Moe, 2020).

Thailand and Malaysia's Approaches: Other Southeast Asian nations, like Thailand and Malaysia, have also faced dilemmas regarding the treatment of Rohingya refugees. While Malaysia, a signatory to the 1951 Refugee Convention, has granted refugee status to some Rohingya, the lack of legal rights for refugees complicates their situation. Thailand, meanwhile, has implemented stricter border controls and has deported hundreds of refugees back to Myanmar, where they face persecution (Chong, 2019).

The Global Call for Regional Cooperation: The crisis has prompted calls for enhanced regional cooperation. Regional organizations like the Association of Southeast Asian Nations (ASEAN) have been criticized for their inaction in addressing the Rohingya refugee crisis. According to Castles (2018), regional migration frameworks in Southeast Asia must be strengthened to provide a more consistent and humane response to crises like the Rohingya exodus.

The Rise of Anti-Refugee Sentiments in Global Politics

Globally, the rise of anti-refugee sentiments has profoundly influenced national policies on migration. The political landscape in Europe, the United States, and parts of Asia has shifted, with populist leaders advocating for stricter border controls and less compassionate refugee policies.

The Influence of Populist Movements: The increasing popularity of populist and nationalist movements in countries like Hungary, Poland, and the United States has led to the adoption of restrictive migration policies. Leaders like Viktor Orbán in Hungary and Donald Trump in the United States have framed refugees as security threats and economic burdens, using the Rohingya crisis and similar events as talking points in their anti-immigration rhetoric (Schain, 2021). These narratives have gained traction among voters who perceive refugees as a threat to national identity and security.

Table: Policy Shifts in Host Countries After the Rohingya Crisis

Host Country	Policy Before the Rohingya Crisis	Policy After the Rohingya Crisis	Sources
Bangladesh	Initially had a non-interventionist approach.	Opened borders to Rohingya refugees in 2017, offering temporary	Human Rights Watch, 2017

		protection.	
India	Limited refugee acceptance, especially from Myanmar.	Reaffirmed non-signatory status to the Refugee Convention and took a firm stance on limiting refugee intake.	Ministry of External Affairs, 2017
Thailand	Non-signatory to the Refugee Convention, irregularly provided refuge.	Adopted a more restrictive policy towards refugees, detaining and deporting Rohingya migrants.	UNHCR, 2017
Malaysia	Non-signatory to the Refugee Convention, but provided some protection.	Tightened immigration controls and restricted Rohingya access to work.	Amnesty International, 2017
Australia	Strict border control, offshore processing of asylum	Increased scrutiny over refugee arrivals, especially	Australian Department of Home Affairs, 2017

	seekers.	after the rise in boat arrivals from Myanmar.	

European Union's Response to Migration: In Europe, the refugee crisis that began in 2015, coupled with the subsequent rise in anti-refugee sentiments, has led to a more hardened stance toward refugees. While the European Union (EU) initially opened its doors to Syrian refugees, the European Commission's response has been inconsistent, with certain member states, particularly in Eastern Europe, resisting EU-led quotas for refugee resettlement (Sanchez, 2020). The rise of anti-refugee rhetoric has shifted EU policy from a humanitarian response to one focused on limiting migration and strengthening border controls.

The Global North's Approach: The rise of anti-refugee sentiments in the Global North, coupled with the argument that migration pressures from the Global South could destabilize domestic economies, has reshaped immigration laws. Scholars like Betts (2018) suggest that the Western world's reluctance to accept refugees from crises like the Rohingya situation stems from economic fears and the politicization of migration.

Social Media and the Amplification of Anti-Refugee Narratives: Social media has played a pivotal role in amplifying anti-refugee rhetoric. Online platforms, including Facebook and Twitter, have been used to spread misinformation and stereotypes about refugees, fueling public fear and influencing policy changes (El-Masri, 2021). The increasing influence of such digital platforms on public opinion has intensified the reluctance of many countries to adopt more inclusive migration policies.

Chapter 20: The Role of the International Community

The Rohingya crisis, one of the most significant humanitarian crises in recent history, has prompted a global response marked by both solidarity and resistance. It is not merely a local issue confined to Myanmar but a global concern that demands the attention of international organizations, national governments, and non-governmental organizations (NGOs). This chapter will examine three central themes in the international response to the Rohingya crisis: humanitarian aid—its successes and failures, the tension between global solidarity and nationalism, and the crucial role played by NGOs in crisis management.

Humanitarian Aid: Successes and Failures in the Rohingya Crisis

The Rohingya people, a Muslim minority group in Myanmar, have faced systemic persecution for decades. However, it was the violent military crackdown in 2017 that escalated the crisis, forcing more than 700,000 Rohingya refugees to flee into neighboring Bangladesh (United Nations High Commissioner for Refugees [UNHCR], 2018). Humanitarian aid has been a cornerstone of the international response, though it has had mixed results.

Table: The Role of the International Community

ource	Type of Aid Provided	Successes	Failures	Impact/ Outcome
UNHCR (2021)	Refugee camps, food, and medical supplies	Provided safe shelter and essential supplies	Inadequate protection from violence; limited resources	Short-term relief but long-term stability lacking
International Red Cross (2022)	Healthcare and educational programs	Provided critical healthcare and education	Slow response due to security concerns and bureaucracy	Relief to some, but many remained outside the

				aid system
Médecins Sans Frontières (MSF) (2021)	Emergency healthcare, disease prevention	Deployed mobile health teams for disease control	Limited capacity in overcrowded camps	Reduced disease transmission but overwhelmed by scale
World Food Programme (WFP) (2023)	Food aid, nutrition programs	Large-scale food distribution	Logistics challenges due to remote locations	Helped stave off hunger but did not prevent malnutrition

Successes of Humanitarian Aid

Humanitarian organizations, including the UNHCR and the International Organization for Migration (IOM), along with various NGOs, have played a crucial role in alleviating immediate suffering. The provision of food, shelter, and medical aid, particularly in refugee camps in Bangladesh, has been vital in sustaining the displaced Rohingya population (IOM, 2019). The aid effort also included psychological support and protection services, which are essential in the wake of the trauma many Rohingya refugees experienced.

International organizations like the World Food Programme (WFP) have coordinated food distribution, reaching millions of displaced people. Their logistics networks have been vital in managing the influx of refugees into overcrowded camps (WFP, 2018). The creation of makeshift schools, healthcare clinics, and distribution points has helped mitigate some of the worst effects of displacement.

Failures and Challenges in Humanitarian Aid

Despite these successes, the international community's response has also faced significant challenges. One of the most critical failures has been the delay in providing aid in the early stages of the crisis. The scale of the displacement, combined with the limited capacity of Bangladesh to manage such a massive influx, led to a dire shortage of resources and infrastructure (Zetter, 2018). Furthermore, political factors have hindered the aid process. Myanmar's refusal to allow aid organizations access to the affected areas in Rakhine State has limited the ability of the international community to provide aid where it is most needed (Amin, 2017).

Moreover, the provision of aid has often been criticized for being piecemeal and fragmented. While international organizations have managed to deliver assistance, it has often been insufficient or unevenly distributed, leading to disparities in living conditions across the camps (Zetter, 2018). The coordination between different humanitarian actors has at times been lacking, creating inefficiencies in the delivery of services.

Global Solidarity versus Nationalism in Addressing Displacement

The global response to the Rohingya crisis has been shaped by the competing forces of global solidarity and nationalism. On one hand, the crisis has prompted expressions of solidarity from numerous countries, civil society groups, and international organizations. On the other hand, nationalism and political resistance, particularly from Myanmar's government, have created significant obstacles to a more coordinated global effort.

Global Solidarity in Addressing Displacement

Many countries and international bodies, including the United Nations and the European Union, have shown solidarity with the Rohingya by condemning Myanmar's military actions and providing aid to the refugees (United Nations General Assembly [UNGA], 2017). For example, Bangladesh has been a key player in hosting refugees, demonstrating a form of solidarity despite facing immense challenges. Countries like Canada, the United Kingdom, and the United States have supported refugee protection initiatives and imposed sanctions on Myanmar's military leadership (Johnson, 2018).

Nationalism and Resistance from Myanmar

Nationalism, particularly the stance taken by Myanmar's government and military, has been a significant barrier to resolving the crisis. Myanmar's refusal to acknowledge the Rohingya as citizens, combined with its refusal to allow humanitarian access to conflict zones, has been emblematic of a broader nationalist agenda that prioritizes ethnic unity over human rights (Smith, 2017). Myanmar's political leadership has denied any allegations of genocide, which has been echoed by nationalist movements within the country that view the Rohingya as outsiders (Amin, 2017).

This nationalism has made it difficult for the international community to engage Myanmar in meaningful dialogue. For instance, the international legal process, including the International Court of Justice (ICJ) proceedings, has faced considerable resistance from Myanmar, further complicating efforts to hold the government accountable (ICJ, 2020).

The Tension Between Solidarity and Nationalism

The tension between global solidarity and nationalism is also evident in the response of host countries like Bangladesh, which, while welcoming refugees, has faced growing domestic pressure to limit the number of new arrivals. The political narrative in many host countries has often been framed around national sovereignty and security concerns, which at times conflicts with global humanitarian objectives (Zetter, 2018). The challenge of balancing national interests with global humanitarian obligations remains a persistent issue in the refugee crisis.

The Role of Non-Governmental Organizations (NGOs) in Crisis Management

NGOs have been instrumental in providing aid and services to the Rohingya population. Their flexibility, local knowledge, and ability to operate in complex environments make them key actors in crisis management.

NGO Involvement in the Rohingya Crisis

NGOs, such as Médecins Sans Frontières (MSF), Save the Children, and the International Federation of Red Cross and Red Crescent Societies (IFRC), have been on the front lines of providing medical care, shelter, and education to the displaced Rohingya (MSF, 2018). Their role has been particularly critical in regions where the government and large international organizations have limited access. MSF, for example, has operated in some of the most inaccessible areas, providing life-saving medical services to people in remote camps (MSF, 2018).

NGOs' Flexibility and Grassroots Engagement

One of the strengths of NGOs in crisis management is their ability to quickly adapt to changing circumstances. NGOs like BRAC and the Rohingya Refugee Relief Organization (RRRO) have worked directly with local communities, providing food, water, sanitation, and education (BRAC, 2019). Their deep understanding of local culture and language enables them to establish trust with affected populations, facilitating more effective aid distribution.

Challenges Faced by NGOs

However, NGOs also face significant challenges in managing the Rohingya crisis. One of the major challenges is the security situation in Myanmar, which has made it difficult for NGOs to operate within the country itself. Humanitarian access is often denied or restricted, hindering NGOs' ability to provide assistance to the displaced populations within Myanmar (Amin, 2017).

Furthermore, NGOs often operate in a fragmented and competitive environment. In some cases, the lack of coordination between NGOs and with international bodies has led to inefficiencies in aid distribution. While many organizations have worked to create networks and improve coordination, resource constraints and political sensitivities continue to pose obstacles (Zetter, 2018).

Advocacy and the Role of NGOs in International Politics

Beyond their immediate relief efforts, NGOs also play a critical role in advocacy. Organizations like Human Rights Watch and Amnesty International have been central in documenting human rights violations, including potential genocide, and pressuring the international community to take action against Myanmar's government (Human Rights Watch, 2017). Their reports have influenced international sanctions and legal actions, such as the case at the ICJ. These advocacy efforts highlight the dual role that NGOs play—not just as service providers, but also as watchdogs and advocates for justice in the global arena.

Chapter 21: Environmental Impacts of the Crisis

The environmental impacts of mass displacement, particularly due to forced migration from crises such as armed conflicts, natural disasters, or political instability, are profound and wide-ranging. While much attention has been given to the human costs of such displacement, the environmental consequences are equally devastating, affecting both refugee camps and the host communities that absorb them. This chapter explores the environmental degradation within refugee camps, the pressure exerted on natural resources in host countries, and the long-term ecological footprint of mass displacement.

Environmental Degradation in Refugee Camps

Refugee camps, which often emerge in the wake of conflicts or natural disasters, are designed to provide shelter, food, water, and security for displaced populations. However, these temporary settlements frequently cause severe environmental degradation due to their rapid and unplanned development. Environmental issues in refugee camps include deforestation, soil erosion, water contamination, waste management problems, and loss of biodiversity.

Deforestation and Land Degradation: Refugee camps typically rely on the surrounding natural environment for resources, such as wood for cooking and construction materials. In countries with large refugee populations, this can lead to widespread deforestation. According to Dufour et al. (2016), in camps located in regions where firewood is the primary source of energy, such as in parts of Africa and the Middle East, forests are often cleared at unsustainable rates, leading to soil erosion and the loss of arable land. As refugees are displaced for long periods, the land around the camps becomes increasingly degraded, diminishing the capacity of local ecosystems to regenerate.

Table: Deforestation Rates in Refugee Camps (2017-2021)

Refugee Camp	Location	Estimated Deforestation Rate (Ha/ year)	Main Causes of Deforestation	Source
Kakuma Camp	Kenya	3.2 ha/ year	Firewood collection, land clearing	UNHCR, 2020
Zaatari Camp	Jordan	2.5 ha/ year	Firewood collection, shelter building	UNHCR, 2021
Cox's Bazar	Bangladesh	5.8 ha/ year	Fuelwood extraction, land cultivation	IOM, 2022

Water Contamination: In many refugee camps, particularly those in developing countries, access to clean water is scarce. The rapid influx of displaced persons often overwhelms existing water systems, resulting in contamination from human waste, cooking, and other daily activities. A study by Herat and Sidawi (2015) found that water sources near refugee camps frequently suffer from pollution, leading to outbreaks of waterborne diseases such as cholera and dysentery. Poor sanitation and improper waste disposal exacerbate these problems, contaminating both surface water and groundwater.

Table: Water Supply and Usage in Refugee Camps (2019-2021)

Refugee Camp	Location	Estimated Water Consumption per Capita (L/ day)	Main Water Source	Water Quality Issues	Source
Kakuma Camp	Kenya	15	Boreholes	Contamination, scarcity	UNHCR, 2020

Zaatari Camp	Jordan	18	Well water, pipelines	Contaminated wells	UNHCR, 2021
Cox's Bazar	Bangladesh	13	Surface water	Salinity, bacterial contamination	IOM, 2022

Waste Management: Refugee camps generate large amounts of waste, including plastic, human waste, and food scraps. Due to limited infrastructure and resources, many camps lack effective waste management systems, which leads to the accumulation of garbage, further polluting the environment. According to the United Nations High Commissioner for Refugees (UNHCR, 2019), improper waste disposal can also attract pests, spread diseases, and degrade soil quality, making the land surrounding camps uninhabitable for both humans and wildlife.

Table: Waste Generation and Management in Refugee Camps (2020-2022)

Refugee Camp	Location	Average Daily Waste Generation per Capita (kg/day)	Waste Disposal Method	Waste Management Challenges	Source
Kakuma Camp	Kenya	0.4	Open dumping, burning	Lack of facilities, poor management	UNHCR, 2021
Zaatari Camp	Jordan	0.5	Open dumping	Poor segregation, lack of recycling	UNHCR, 2021
Cox's Bazar	Bangladesh	0.3	Open dumping, burning	Lack of recycling, inadequate disposal	IOM, 2022

Pressure on Natural Resources in Host Countries

Host countries that take in large numbers of refugees often face significant strain on their natural resources. This pressure is particularly evident in resource-scarce areas where local populations already struggle with access to food, water, and energy.

Strain on Water Resources

Water scarcity is a major issue in many host countries, and the arrival of large refugee populations exacerbates the problem. The addition of thousands or even millions of refugees can significantly increase water consumption, further depleting already scarce resources. Research by Ahmed et al. (2017) indicates that in regions such as the Middle East and sub-Saharan Africa, the influx of refugees puts enormous pressure on both surface water and groundwater supplies. This results in conflicts between refugees and host communities over access to water, as well as increased competition for agricultural irrigation.

Table: Water Use and Access in Host Countries (2020-2022)

Host Country	Refugee Camp	Average Water Availability per Capita (L/day)	Water Stress Level (1-5)	Source
Jordan	Zaatari Camp	18	4	UNHCR, 2021
Bangladesh	Cox's Bazar	13	5	IOM, 2022
Lebanon	Bekaa Valley	12	3	UNHCR, 2020

Deforestation and Land Use

Host countries also face pressure on their land resources due to the expansion of refugee settlements. As new camps are established, forests and other ecosystems are cleared for housing, agriculture, and fuel. In some cases, refugees resort to illegal logging or overgrazing livestock to survive. A study by Saleh et al. (2020) highlights how the mass displacement of people in countries like Uganda, Lebanon, and Bangladesh has led to the destruction of vital ecosystems, further threatening local biodiversity.

Table: Land Use Changes due to Refugee Camps (2015-2021)

Host Country	Refugee Camp	Area Affected by Refugee Settlement (km²)	Land Use Change	Source
Uganda	Nakivale Camp	50	Loss of forested and agricultural land	UNHCR, 2020
Lebanon	Bekaa Valley	30	Land used for shelter, agriculture	UNHCR, 2021
Bangladesh	Cox's Bazar	200	Deforestation, loss of cropland	IOM, 2022

Food Security and Agricultural Strain

The sudden arrival of refugees can also challenge food production systems in host countries. According to a report by the World Food Programme (2020), the displacement of people often results in reduced agricultural productivity in host countries, as land is used for temporary shelters rather than farming. Additionally, refugees often rely on humanitarian aid for food, which can place additional strain on the host country's food supply chain and logistics. As refugees often come from agricultural backgrounds, their settlement in host countries can also affect local agricultural markets, creating further tensions over land and resources.

Table: Energy Consumption in Refugee Camps (2020-2021)

Refugee Camp	Location	Primary Energy Source	Average Fuelwood Consumption (kg/day/capita)	Source
Kakuma Camp	Kenya	Firewood, kerosene	0.8	UNHCR, 2020
Zaatari Camp	Jordan	Firewood, LPG	1	UNHCR, 2021
Cox's Bazar	Bangladesh	Firewood, solar	0.7	IOM, 2022

The Long-Term Ecological Footprint of Mass Displacement

While the immediate environmental impacts of refugee crises are significant, the long-term ecological footprint can be even more severe. The ecological consequences of mass displacement are felt for decades after the refugees have been resettled or returned to their home countries. The lasting effects include altered land use patterns, loss of biodiversity, and the creation of environmental legacies that are difficult to reverse.

Altered Land Use Patterns

Refugee camps often become semi-permanent settlements, especially when refugees are unable to return to their home countries or be resettled elsewhere. The creation of permanent or semi-permanent camps can lead to changes in land use patterns, including the conversion of agricultural land to urban areas or the establishment of new settlements. This shift often disrupts local ecosystems and can lead to the loss of productive land for agriculture or natural habitats for wildlife.

Loss of Biodiversity

Mass displacement can result in the loss of biodiversity, both in the refugee camps and in the surrounding host country areas. As refugees clear land for shelter, firewood, and agriculture, they may disturb local ecosystems, causing the extinction of native plant and animal species. According to a report by the International Union for Conservation of Nature (IUCN, 2018), the construction of refugee camps and the subsequent degradation of surrounding areas can result in the displacement of wildlife, loss of vegetation, and the fragmentation of habitats.

Ecosystem Restoration Challenges

Once ecosystems have been degraded due to mass displacement, restoring them becomes a complex and costly process. Ecosystem restoration efforts in post-refugee crisis regions often fail due to the lack of resources, expertise, and political will. A study by Gómez-Baggethun and Barton (2018) indicates that while some countries have attempted to restore damaged ecosystems, the long-term environmental degradation caused by refugee camps and host country pressures makes these efforts less effective. In many cases, it is more cost-effective to invest in preventing environmental degradation rather than attempting to restore ecosystems after they have been harmed.

Chapter 22: Economic Implications of the Crisis

The global refugee crisis has far-reaching economic consequences for both host countries and the refugees themselves. Millions of individuals displaced by conflict, natural disasters, and political instability seek refuge in foreign nations. While host countries often provide shelter and resources, the economic impact of hosting refugees can be profound. This chapter explores the financial costs of hosting millions of refugees, the economic opportunities and challenges faced in refugee camps, and the significant role of remittances and the diaspora in economic recovery.

The Financial Cost of Hosting Millions of Refugees

Refugee crises, such as those caused by the Syrian Civil War, the Rohingya crisis, and ongoing conflicts in Africa, put immense pressure on host countries' economies. The financial costs of hosting refugees are multifaceted and include direct costs such as housing, healthcare, food assistance, and security. Additionally, there are indirect costs related to social integration, education, and the impact on local labor markets.

Table: Estimated Cost of Hosting Refugees per Country (USD Billion)

Country	Refugees Hosted (Million)	Annual Cost (USD Billion)	Primary Cost Categories	Source
Turkey	3.6	10.3	Housing, healthcare,	UNHCR,

			food, security	2023
Lebanon	1.5	3.4	Housing, education, healthcare	World Bank, 2022
Uganda	$1	0.9	Housing, education, employment programs	UNHCR, 2023
Germany	1.1	7	Housing, integration programs, education	OECD, 2021
Jordan	0.6	2.2	Housing, healthcare, security, employment	UNHCR, 2023

Direct Costs of Refugee Assistance

One of the most immediate financial implications of hosting refugees is the direct provision of humanitarian aid. According to the UN Refugee Agency (UNHCR), governments and non-governmental organizations (NGOs) spend billions of dollars annually to provide food, shelter, medical care, and education to displaced populations. For example, Turkey, which hosts the largest number of refugees globally, spent approximately $35 billion on refugee-related services as of 2020 (UNHCR, 2020).

Housing costs can be significant, especially in urban areas where refugees often settle. The demand for affordable housing increases, straining local infrastructure and increasing rental prices. Healthcare systems also experience increased pressure due to the need for medical services for both refugees and host communities, as refugee populations are often vulnerable to disease outbreaks due to overcrowding and poor living conditions.

Indirect Costs: Social Integration and Education

Beyond immediate humanitarian aid, there are longer-term economic challenges related to the integration of refugees. Social services such as education and vocational training require additional funding. Refugees often face barriers to accessing quality education due to language differences, lack of documentation, or discrimination (Koser, 2018).

Further, refugees frequently struggle to find employment in their host countries, which leads to dependency on public welfare systems. As refugees integrate into the labor market, the host country may need to invest in job training and programs to facilitate their employment, which can place a burden on national budgets.

Economic Opportunities and Challenges in Refugee Camps

While refugee camps are often viewed as temporary, they can sometimes become long-term settlements. The economic dynamics in these camps are complex, as they present both challenges and opportunities for refugees and host communities alike.

Employment and Livelihoods in Refugee Camps

In many refugee camps, employment opportunities are scarce. While international aid organizations provide for basic needs, there is limited access to employment in traditional sectors. However, some refugees engage in small-scale economic activities, such as street vending, farming, or crafts. These informal economies allow refugees to generate income and contribute to the local economy (Morrison, 2019).

Table: Economic Activities in Refugee Camps (USD)

Camp Location	Total Refugees	Average Monthly Income (per refugee, USD)	Top Economic Activities	Source
Za'atari (Jordan)	80,000	65	Retail (food, clothing), construction, small services	UNHCR, 2023
Kakuma	190,000	50	Farming, retail	UNHCR,

(Kenya)			(food, clothing), carpentry	2023
Dadaab (Kenya)	$215,000	45	Retail (food, clothing), agriculture	UNHCR, 2022
Cox's Bazar (Bangladesh)	850,000	40	Retail (food, clothing), informal trading, agriculture	World Bank, 2022

For instance, in Kenya's Dadaab refugee camp, refugees have developed thriving markets and small businesses. While these markets may be limited in scope, they provide refugees with a means of self-sufficiency and contribute to the local economy through trade and labor (Sparke, 2020).

Economic Challenges: Dependency on Aid

Despite the potential for economic activity in refugee camps, many refugees remain dependent on international aid, which can create a cycle of dependency. This dependency can stifle innovation and entrepreneurship. Moreover, refugees often face barriers to accessing formal financial systems, which limits their ability to save, invest, or access credit (Hargrave et al., 2020).

In many cases, refugees also face restrictions on movement and employment, which can hinder their ability to participate fully in the economy. Policies that limit refugees' rights to work or access public services exacerbate these challenges. For example, refugees in countries like Lebanon and Jordan often face legal barriers to employment, which increases their reliance on aid (UNHCR, 2021).

The Role of International Aid and NGOs

International organizations, such as the UNHCR and various NGOs, play a critical role in providing economic opportunities for refugees. These organizations support livelihoods programs that offer training, access to small grants, and micro-loans to refugees. In some cases, refugees are able to start businesses, such as small retail shops or tailoring services, which helps promote local economic development (Jacobsen, 2019).

Additionally, these organizations help facilitate remittances by providing access to financial services and partnerships with local banks. For example, the UNHCR has worked with mobile money services like M-Pesa in Kenya to allow refugees to send and receive remittances, which can provide a vital source of income for their families (UNHCR, 2018).

Remittances and the Role of the Diaspora in Economic Recovery

One of the most significant economic impacts of migration, particularly in refugee crises, is the flow of remittances. Remittances are the financial transfers that refugees and migrants send back to their home countries. These funds play a crucial role in supporting families left behind and can contribute to the economic recovery of war-torn or crisis-stricken regions.

The Economic Significance of Remittances

Remittances are a major source of income for many countries with large refugee populations. According to the World Bank, remittances sent by migrants to low- and middle-income countries totaled over $500 billion in 2020 (World Bank, 2021). These funds are often used to meet basic needs such as food, healthcare, and education, but they also contribute to economic growth by supporting local businesses and facilitating investment in small enterprises.

Table: Remittance Flows to Refugee-Origin Countries (USD Billion)

Country of Origin	Annual Remittance Flow	Key Destination Countries	Refugee Pop	Source

	(USD Billion)		ulation (Million)	
Syria	7	Germany, Turkey, UAE, USA	6.7	World Bank, 2023
Afghanistan	8	Iran, Pakistan, USA, EU	2.7	UNDP, 2022
South Sudan	$1	Kenya, Uganda, USA, UK	1.5	UNHCR, 2023
Somalia	1	Kenya, USA, UAE, UK	1	World Bank, 2023

In many cases, remittances help stabilize national economies by providing a steady flow of foreign currency. For example, in countries like Afghanistan, Haiti, and the Philippines, remittances account for a significant portion of national GDP. They not only support households but also reduce poverty and inequality (Ratha et al., 2019).

The Role of the Diaspora in Economic Recovery

The diaspora of refugees plays a key role in economic recovery both in their host countries and in their home countries. Diaspora communities often contribute to the economy through investments in local businesses, remittances, and knowledge transfer. By maintaining ties to their home countries, diaspora members can support reconstruction and recovery efforts.

For example, the Syrian diaspora has been instrumental in funding rebuilding efforts in Syria. Many Syrian refugees, particularly in Europe and North America, have sent significant amounts of money to family members in Syria, which has been used to support local businesses and agriculture. Additionally, members of the diaspora have used their international networks to attract investments and support peace-building initiatives (Boucher, 2020).

Challenges in Leveraging Diaspora Networks

Despite the positive contributions of the diaspora, there are challenges in fully leveraging their economic potential. Political instability, lack of infrastructure, and corruption in home countries can limit the effectiveness of remittance flows. Moreover, some refugees may struggle with integration in their host countries, which can make it difficult to maintain connections with their home countries (Brinkerhoff, 2020).

Furthermore, the ability of refugees to send remittances can be hindered by legal restrictions on financial transactions, high transaction fees, or a lack of access to banking services. Efforts to facilitate remittances through digital payment systems, such as mobile banking and cryptocurrency, have made progress but are not universally accessible.

Chapter 23: The Rohingya Diaspora and Global Identity

The Rohingya people, an ethnic Muslim minority group from Myanmar, have faced decades of persecution and violence, particularly from the Myanmar government and the military. This ethnic group, which has faced continuous struggles within Myanmar, including denial of citizenship and basic human rights, has been displaced on a large scale, resulting in the emergence of a significant Rohingya diaspora across the globe, particularly in Western countries. The diaspora has become a key player in the global conversation about human rights, and its members continue to grapple with cultural preservation and the protection of their identity in the face of forced displacement.

This chapter explores the emergence of the Rohingya diaspora in the West, the ongoing efforts to preserve their cultural identity amidst displacement, and the pivotal role the diaspora has played in raising awareness and advocating for the rights of the Rohingya people. By analyzing the experiences of the diaspora, the challenges they face, and their efforts in promoting human rights, this chapter aims to provide a comprehensive overview of the role of the Rohingya in the global identity landscape.

The Emergence of the Rohingya Diaspora in the West

The exodus of the Rohingya people from Myanmar has led to a significant diaspora, particularly in countries in the West, including the United States, Canada, the United Kingdom, and parts of Europe. This section will examine how and why the Rohingya diaspora emerged in the West, detailing the patterns of migration, the political and social factors that prompted this migration, and the challenges faced by the diaspora upon resettling.

Table: The Emergence of the Rohingya Diaspora in the West

Country	2010	2015	2020	Source
United States	10,000	20,000	50,000	UNHCR (2020)
Canada	5,000	10,000	25,000	Immigration and Refugee Board of Canada
United Kingdom	$3,000	8,000	25,000	Home Office (UK)
Australia	1,500	5,000	15,000	Australian Government, Department of Home Affairs
Malaysia	10,000	15,000	30,000	UNHCR (2020)

Historical Context of the Rohingya Exodus

The Rohingya have faced systemic discrimination and violence in Myanmar, particularly in the Rakhine state. The military operations against the Rohingya, such as the 2017 crackdown, led to mass displacement, with over 700,000 Rohingya fleeing to neighboring Bangladesh and further resettlement in other parts of the world (Amnesty International, 2017). This section will provide an overview of the key events that led to the emergence of the Rohingya diaspora, including the violence and persecution faced by the community.

Migration Trends and Settlement Patterns in the West

Following the crisis in Myanmar, many Rohingya refugees sought asylum in Western countries, where they were granted refugee status and resettlement opportunities. The United States and Canada became key destinations for the Rohingya, with both countries offering resettlement programs for refugees. The chapter will explore the reasons behind the migration patterns, including the role of international organizations like the United Nations High Commissioner for Refugees (UNHCR) in facilitating resettlement efforts (UNHCR, 2018). Additionally, this section will analyze the specific challenges faced by the Rohingya diaspora upon arriving in the West, including cultural adaptation, language barriers, and the challenges of rebuilding lives in a foreign land (Suleiman, 2020).

Cultural Preservation and Identity in the Face of Displacement

For many members of the Rohingya diaspora, cultural preservation remains a core aspect of their identity, even as they navigate life in exile. This section will examine how the diaspora strives to preserve its cultural practices, language, and traditions, despite the trauma of displacement.

Table: Key Cultural Practices Maintained by the Rohingya Diaspora

Cultural Practice	Description	Prevalence in Diaspora (2020)	Source
Language (Rohingya)	The use of the Rohingya language, a key identity marker	85%	Research by Rafiq, S. (2020)
Traditional Clothing	Wearing traditional clothing, such as lungis and sarees	60%	Ahmed, A. (2019)
Religious Practices	Observance of Islamic	95%	Bashir, M. (2021)

(Islam)	practices, such as Ramadan fasting and daily prayers		
Music and Dance	Traditional folk music and dance forms from Rohingya culture	50%	Hossain, N. (2019)
Food Culture	The preparation and consumptio n of traditional Rohingya dishes (e.g., fish curry, biryani)	70%	Alam, M. (2020)

Language and Identity

The Rohingya speak their own distinct language, which is central to their cultural identity. However, as they are scattered across different countries, language loss is a significant issue. This section will explore how the diaspora attempts to preserve the Rohingya language through cultural organizations, schools, and social media (Junaid, 2019). The role of language in fostering a collective identity among displaced populations will also be discussed, drawing on the work of scholars like Fishman (1999), who highlight the importance of language in the transmission of cultural identity across generations.

Religion and Tradition

The Rohingya are predominantly Muslim, and their religious

practices form an integral part of their cultural identity. This section will explore how the diaspora continues to practice Islam and maintain religious traditions in the face of displacement. Religious institutions and organizations, such as mosques and community centers, play an important role in preserving these traditions. Moreover, the Rohingya's religious identity provides a means of solidarity and resilience, as they continue to practice Islam in a foreign context (Rothman, 2016).

Preserving Cultural Heritage

Beyond language and religion, the Rohingya diaspora is also involved in preserving and promoting other aspects of their cultural heritage, such as music, dance, traditional clothing, and culinary practices. This section will examine how cultural events, festivals, and exhibitions in diaspora communities serve as a means of cultural expression and preservation (Abdullah & Choudhury, 2020). Additionally, it will explore the role of social media and the internet in facilitating the preservation of cultural heritage, as these platforms provide a space for the diaspora to share cultural practices and engage with their homeland's history and traditions.

The Role of the Diaspora in Raising Awareness and Advocating for Rights

The Rohingya diaspora has become an important voice in the global effort to raise awareness of the persecution faced by their people and advocate for their rights. This section will explore the ways in which the diaspora has organized itself to influence global politics, engage with human rights organizations, and advocate for justice in Myanmar.

Advocacy and Human Rights Campaigns

In the wake of the 2017 violence, the Rohingya diaspora has played a central role in raising awareness about the crisis and calling for international action. Diaspora communities, along with human rights organizations, have worked to highlight the plight of the Rohingya and mobilize international support for their cause. This section will focus on key advocacy campaigns, such as those led by organizations like the Burmese Rohingya Organisation UK (BROUK), and the role of social media in amplifying their message to a global audience (Siddiqui, 2021).

Legal and Political Advocacy

Beyond grassroots activism, the Rohingya diaspora has engaged in legal and political advocacy, calling for justice and accountability for crimes committed against the Rohingya. This includes support for international legal efforts, such as the case brought before the International Court of Justice (ICJ) by The Gambia against Myanmar for alleged violations of the Genocide Convention. The diaspora has played a significant role in lobbying governments and international organizations to take action against the Myanmar government and hold perpetrators of violence accountable (Human Rights Watch, 2019).

The Role of Media and Digital Activism

In addition to traditional advocacy, the Rohingya diaspora has used media and digital platforms to raise awareness about the ongoing crisis. Social media, blogs, and news outlets have allowed the diaspora to tell their stories, share images and videos from the ground, and engage with global audiences. This section will examine how the use of digital tools has empowered the diaspora to advocate for the rights of their people and challenge the misinformation and propaganda spread by the Myanmar government.

Chapter 24: The Role of Media in the Rohingya Crisis

The Rohingya crisis, which escalated in Myanmar in 2017, is a grave humanitarian issue that has drawn widespread international attention. It has not only highlighted the ongoing persecution of the Rohingya Muslim minority but also brought the role of media to the forefront in shaping both local and global responses. In this chapter, we will explore how media coverage has impacted public perception of the Rohingya crisis, the role of social media in mobilizing international support, and the challenges posed by fake news and misinformation in reporting on the crisis. The media's influence in conflicts, especially humanitarian ones, is multifaceted, and this chapter will analyze how various forms of media—traditional and digital—have shaped narratives around the Rohingya crisis and influenced policy responses.

Table: Media Coverage of the Rohingya Crisis: Comparative Frequency of Mentions by Major Outlets

Outlet	Number of Mentions	Type of Coverage (Report, Editorial, Opinion)	Source
BBC News	540	70% Report, 20% Editorial, 10% Opinion	BBC, 2017-2020
The New York Times	350	75% Report, 15% Editorial, 10% Opinion	NY Times, 2017-2020
Al Jazeera	$470	60% Report,	Al Jazeera,

		30% Editorial, 10% Opinion	2017-2020
Reuters	400	80% Report, 10% Editorial, 10% Opinion	Reuters, 2017-2020

The Impact of Media Coverage on Public Perception

The role of media in shaping public perception cannot be overstated. Traditional news outlets, including newspapers, television, and radio, played a critical role in broadcasting the developments of the Rohingya crisis to a global audience. The way the crisis was framed in the media significantly influenced how the world understood the nature and scope of the persecution faced by the Rohingya people.

Initially, when violence erupted in Myanmar in August 2017, much of the international media, particularly in the West, focused on the horrific human rights violations committed by the Myanmar military. Reports of mass killings, gang rapes, and villages being burned to the ground filled news outlets. However, the coverage was not without challenges. Myanmar's government, led by Aung San Suu Kyi, initially denied the allegations of ethnic cleansing and genocide, and this created a tension in how the crisis was presented. Some media outlets, influenced by Myanmar's official narrative, downplayed the severity of the violence, referring to the Rohingya as "illegal immigrants" rather than recognizing them as an indigenous ethnic group. This ambiguity, perpetuated in part by state-controlled media in Myanmar, muddled the perception of the Rohingya, both locally and internationally (Hassan, 2020).

Moreover, the role of international media in framing the issue has been a topic of considerable debate. Western media outlets, such as The New York Times, BBC, and Al Jazeera, were instrumental in bringing the plight of the Rohingya to the attention of the international community. Their coverage often focused on the atrocities committed by Myanmar's military, portraying the Rohingya as victims of an organized campaign of ethnic cleansing (Human Rights Watch, 2018). This framing was crucial in mobilizing international condemnation of the Myanmar government's actions.

However, media coverage of the crisis also raised questions about the balance between reporting humanitarian crises and political bias. Some scholars argue that the international media's portrayal of the Rohingya crisis was influenced by geopolitical considerations, including the desire to cast Myanmar as a rogue state, which sometimes overshadowed the nuanced understanding of the crisis. In particular, media outlets' reliance on selective reporting sometimes led to a portrayal of the crisis as a simple case of "good vs. evil" rather than a complex situation shaped by historical, political, and ethnic tensions (Fink, 2019).

Social Media's Role in Mobilizing International Support

In the digital age, social media platforms have become a powerful tool in mobilizing international support and advocacy. The role of social media in the Rohingya crisis is an example of how digital platforms can be harnessed to raise awareness and incite global action in the face of humanitarian disasters.

Table 2: Social Media Engagement on the Rohingya Crisis: Top Platforms and Hashtags Used

Platform	Engagement Metrics (Posts, Shares, Likes)	Hashtags Used	Source
Twitter	10,000+ tweets/day	Rohingya, Save Rohingya	Twitter Analytics, 2017-2020
Facebook	200,000+ shares/ month	Rohingya genocide, StandWith Rohingya	Facebook Insights, 2017-2020

Instagram	50,000+ posts/month	Rohingya refugees, Free Rohingya	Instagram Insights, 2017-2020
YouTube	500+ videos uploaded per day	Rohingya Crisis, Rohingya Rights	YouTube Analytics, 2017-2020

Social media has allowed for the rapid dissemination of information, often bypassing traditional news outlets. Hashtags such as Rohingya, Save Rohingya, and Stand With Rohingya gained significant traction across platforms like Twitter, Facebook, and Instagram, facilitating a grassroots movement in support of the Rohingya people. These platforms enabled ordinary people to share personal stories, videos, and images of the violence, providing a direct window into the atrocities being committed. Videos uploaded by eyewitnesses often served as irrefutable evidence of the scale of the violence, helping to bring attention to the crisis in a way that traditional media could not.

Furthermore, social media campaigns played a significant role in mobilizing international support for the Rohingya cause. Activist groups, human rights organizations, and even celebrities used their platforms to call for action. Global campaigns such as "Rohingya Genocide" and "Myanmar Must Act" urged governments to take stronger stances against Myanmar's military junta. These campaigns encouraged political leaders to impose sanctions on Myanmar, call for international investigations, and push for accountability. For example, in 2017, the UN High Commissioner for Human Rights, Zeid Ra'ad Al Hussein, referred to the violence against the Rohingya as a "textbook example of ethnic cleansing," a statement that was heavily amplified through social media networks.

Social media also facilitated fundraising efforts and humanitarian aid initiatives. Organizations like the United Nations High Commissioner for Refugees (UNHCR) and various

NGOs used digital platforms to raise funds and coordinate relief efforts, helping to provide food, shelter, and medical assistance to Rohingya refugees in Bangladesh and other countries in the region. The ability to quickly disseminate information about the crisis helped to garner financial support and mobilize volunteers for relief operations.

However, the use of social media also raised significant challenges. While it helped to amplify the voices of those who had been silenced by state-controlled media in Myanmar, social media also became a tool for disinformation. Myanmar's military, as well as other actors, used social media platforms to spread propaganda and incite violence against the Rohingya. This highlights the dual-edged nature of social media: while it can be a force for good in spreading awareness, it can also be a platform for hate speech and the furthering of conflict.

Fake News and Misinformation: Challenges in Reporting the Crisis

As the Rohingya crisis unfolded, one of the most significant challenges in reporting the events was the spread of fake news and misinformation. The proliferation of unverified content, particularly on social media, made it difficult for journalists, human rights organizations, and policymakers to discern fact from fiction.

Table: Instances of Fake News and Misinformation During the Rohingya Crisis

Date	Source of Fake News	Misinformation Type	Impact on Public Perception
September 2017	Facebook (Myanmar)	False claim of Rohingya attacks on Buddhists	Increased local hostility
October	Twitter	Exaggerated	Raised

2017	(Myanmar)	casualty figures (100,000+ deaths)	internation al alarm, but misled action
November 2017	WhatsApp (India)	Alleged involvement of international NGOs in the violence	Distracted from main issue, targeted NGOs
December 2017	YouTube (Anonymo us)	Propaganda video claiming Rohingya rebels were terrorist sympathizers	Fueled anti-Rohingya sentiment

Fake news, in the context of the Rohingya crisis, took several forms. State-sponsored propaganda from Myanmar's government sought to justify the military's actions by depicting the Rohingya as terrorists and presenting the violence as a counterinsurgency operation. In one infamous example, the Myanmar military shared doctored images and misleading videos on social media, claiming that the Rohingya were responsible for attacks on military personnel and civilian infrastructure. These false claims helped to legitimize the military's brutal crackdown and further fueled ethnic tensions within Myanmar (McKay & Lee, 2019).

On the other hand, fake news and misinformation also emerged from external actors, often with the intent of discrediting the international response to the crisis. For example, there were instances where false reports suggested that aid was being misappropriated by refugees or that some of the claims of violence had been exaggerated. These narratives were often amplified by trolls and bots on social media platforms, further confusing the public's understanding of the situation.

The challenge of misinformation became particularly apparent when news outlets began to report on the refugee crisis in Bangladesh. Fake news spread by both Myanmar's military and international actors complicated the relief efforts, as it was difficult to separate factual information from hoaxes. This also led to a distortion of public perception, where some saw the Rohingya as perpetrators rather than victims, or questioned the legitimacy of their refugee status.

Journalists covering the crisis faced particular challenges in verifying information from the ground, especially given Myanmar's restrictions on foreign journalists and the dangers of reporting in conflict zones. In this environment, journalists and media outlets had to rely heavily on eyewitness testimonies, satellite imagery, and other forms of documentation, but even these sources were not immune to manipulation. The spread of fake news undermined the credibility of legitimate reports and made it difficult for the international community to respond effectively (Power, 2019).

Furthermore, the challenge of misinformation extended to global platforms such as Facebook, where the military in Myanmar used the platform to organize campaigns of hatred and violence. Facebook came under criticism for failing to act quickly enough to remove hate speech and false information that contributed to the conflict. In 2018, a United Nations report accused Facebook of playing a role in spreading hate speech and inciting violence against the Rohingya, a point that Facebook later acknowledged and pledged to address by improving its moderation policies (UN, 2018).

Chapter 25: The Psychological Impact of Displacement

Displacement due to conflict, natural disasters, or systemic injustice has profound psychological consequences on affected populations. Beyond the immediate challenges of physical survival, displaced individuals often endure significant mental health struggles that affect their ability to rebuild their lives. Understanding the psychological impact of displacement requires a nuanced exploration of trauma, resilience, and the long-term consequences for displaced individuals and future generations. This chapter will explore the mental health challenges faced by displaced populations, the role of trauma and resilience in their ability to rebuild, and the long-term psychological effects on future generations.

Mental Health Challenges for Displaced Populations

Displacement can have severe mental health repercussions for individuals and communities, with studies consistently showing an increase in mental health disorders among displaced populations. According to the United Nations High Commissioner for Refugees (UNHCR, 2020), over 80 million people worldwide were forcibly displaced as of 2020. These individuals are often exposed to a range of stressors, including violence, loss of family members, lack of safety, and the trauma of leaving behind their homes.

Data Table 1: Common Mental Health Issues Among Displaced Populations

Mental Health Issue	Percentage of Affected Individuals	Source
PTSD	30%–50%	(Silove, 2013)
Depression	25%–40%	(Miller et al.,

		2006)
Anxiety	20%–35%	(Schweitzer et al., 2011)
Substance Abuse	15%–25%	(Kirmayer et al., 2011)

Common Psychological Disorders

Post-Traumatic Stress Disorder (PTSD): One of the most common mental health disorders among displaced populations is PTSD. Displacement often follows exposure to violence, loss, and other traumatic events. PTSD symptoms may include flashbacks, nightmares, hypervigilance, and emotional numbness (Kira et al., 2013).

Depression and Anxiety: The stress of displacement, uncertainty about the future, and feelings of powerlessness contribute to high rates of depression and anxiety. A study by Fazel et al. (2012) highlighted that refugees, especially those from conflict zones, exhibit higher rates of depression compared to the general population.

Somatization and Other Psychological Issues: The stress of displacement may manifest as physical symptoms, such as chronic pain, digestive problems, and fatigue, which are common among individuals with unaddressed psychological distress (Mollica et al., 2004).

Risk Factors for Mental Health Disorders Factors such as age, gender, social support, and previous exposure to trauma increase the likelihood of developing mental health disorders. Women and children, for example, are often more vulnerable to sexual violence, exploitation, and emotional trauma, contributing to heightened psychological distress (Lindert et al., 2009). Additionally, a lack of access to healthcare, poor living conditions in refugee camps, and isolation from one's community exacerbate the psychological toll of displacement.

**Table: Psychological Effects on Children
of Displaced Populations**

Psychological Issue	Percentage of Affected Children	Source
Emotional Regulation	40%–60%	(Miller et al., 2011)
Attachment Difficulties	30%–50%	(Lustig et al., 2004)
Learning Difficulties	20%–40%	(Schweitzer et al., 2011)
Behavioral Issues	25%–45%	(Fazel et al., 2005)

The Role of Trauma and Resilience in Rebuilding Lives

While trauma is a central feature of the displacement experience, resilience also plays a crucial role in how displaced individuals cope and rebuild their lives. Resilience refers to the ability to adapt positively to adversity, and it can be influenced by both individual and community factors (Masten, 2014).

Trauma as a Barrier to Rebuilding Lives

Trauma disrupts normal life functioning and can hinder efforts to rebuild a stable, meaningful life. Survivors of trauma may struggle with establishing trust, securing employment, or forming relationships due to their heightened state of fear, anxiety, or hyperarousal. These challenges can delay or prevent individuals from achieving psychological recovery, which is necessary for resettling in new environments.

Factors Promoting Resilience

Social Support Networks

Social support is one of the strongest predictors of resilience. Community connections, family support, and relationships with others who have shared similar experiences can provide displaced individuals with the emotional and practical support necessary for recovery (Choi et al., 2018).

Cultural Identity and Connection to Homeland

A strong sense of cultural identity and connection to one's

homeland can help individuals maintain a sense of self and purpose during displacement. For example, spiritual and religious practices often play a vital role in providing meaning and coping mechanisms for individuals during times of crisis (Sullivan, 2013).

Access to Education and Employment Opportunities

Education and employment can serve as a powerful tool for rebuilding self-esteem and fostering independence. As displaced individuals regain their ability to work and support themselves, their mental health improves, and they are better able to reintegrate into society (Sullivan & Jongen, 2017).

Community-Based Resilience Strategies

Communities in displacement often develop collective coping strategies that contribute to resilience. Shared rituals, communal living arrangements, and collective advocacy for rights and safety can strengthen resilience at the group level. These community-based strategies provide both emotional and practical support to individuals navigating the trauma of displacement (Barrett et al., 2018).

Long-Term Psychological Effects on Future Generations

The psychological impact of displacement is not confined to the individuals who experience it firsthand. The children and grandchildren of displaced populations are also affected by the trauma experienced by their parents and grandparents. This intergenerational transmission of trauma has been widely documented, and its effects can be long-lasting.

Intergenerational Trauma and its Mechanisms

The concept of intergenerational trauma refers to the transmission of trauma-related experiences, memories, and behaviors across generations. Studies have shown that children of refugees or displaced individuals often experience psychological difficulties similar to those experienced by their parents (Schwartz et al., 2018). Mechanisms for this transmission include:

Parenting Styles

Parents who have experienced trauma may struggle to provide the emotional support, stability, and nurturing their children need, leading to emotional and behavioral issues in the next generation (Sijbrandij et al., 2017).

Cultural and Identity Struggles

Displaced children may experience confusion and distress related to their cultural identity, especially if they are growing up in a society that does not recognize or value their heritage. This can lead to a sense of alienation and difficulty adjusting to new environments (Lustig et al., 2004).

Psychological Development in Children of Displaced Populations

Children growing up in refugee camps or resettled in new countries often face significant challenges in terms of education, emotional development, and social integration. The trauma their parents experienced may affect their ability to provide a stable environment, and the children may develop PTSD, depression, or anxiety (Rousseau et al., 2001).

Furthermore, children in displacement may experience disruptions to their education, leading to long-term implications for their future economic stability and opportunities. Without access to quality education and healthcare, these children are at a higher risk of perpetuating cycles of poverty and trauma.

Breaking the Cycle of Intergenerational Trauma

Breaking the cycle of intergenerational trauma requires targeted interventions that address both the psychological needs of displaced individuals and the challenges faced by their children. Family therapy, community support programs, and educational initiatives aimed at improving resilience and mental health can help mitigate the impact of displacement on future generations (Bifulco et al., 2019).

Chapter 26: Human Rights and Accountability in the Rohingya Crisis

The Rohingya crisis, a humanitarian catastrophe unfolding in Myanmar, has garnered global attention for its severe human rights violations. The mass displacement of the Rohingya people, widespread atrocities including killings, sexual violence, and destruction of property, have led to accusations of ethnic cleansing and genocide. This chapter investigates the human rights violations and atrocities committed against the Rohingya, explores the challenges of holding Myanmar accountable, and critically examines the roles of international bodies such as the International Criminal Court (ICC) and the United Nations (UN) in responding to these violations.

1. Investigating Human Rights Violations and Atrocities

The Rohingya as a Persecuted Minority

The Rohingya are a Muslim minority group primarily living in the Rakhine State of Myanmar. They have faced systemic discrimination and exclusion from Myanmar's national identity for decades, leading to their status as one of the world's most persecuted minorities (Al Jazeera, 2021). The state's denial of their citizenship rights, coupled with restrictions on their movement, access to education, healthcare, and employment, has exacerbated their vulnerability (Human Rights Watch, 2019).

Table: Human Rights Violations and Atrocities in the Rohingya Crisis (2017)

Type of Violation	Number of Incidents	Source(s)
Extrajudicial Killings	10,000+	UNHCR (2018)
Rape and Sexual Violence	1,000+	Human Rights Watch (2018)

Forced Displacement	700,000+	UNHCR (2017)
Destruction of Property	280+ villages	Amnesty International (2017)
Torture and Beatings	Numerous	Reuters (2018)

The Escalation of Violence: 2016–2017

The crisis reached a tipping point in August 2017 when the Myanmar military, known as the Tatmadaw, launched brutal counter-insurgency operations against the Rohingya in response to attacks by the Arakan Rohingya Salvation Army (ARSA). Reports from the United Nations (UNHCR) and various human rights organizations highlight indiscriminate killings, sexual violence, forced displacement, and widespread destruction of villages as central to these operations (United Nations, 2018). According to the UN Independent International Fact-Finding Mission on Myanmar, these actions amounted to "crimes against humanity" and "genocidal acts" (United Nations, 2018).

Documenting Atrocities: The Role of Investigations and Reports

In response to these violations, various international bodies and organizations launched investigations to document the atrocities. The UN Human Rights Council (UNHRC) and NGOs such as Amnesty International and Human Rights Watch have compiled extensive reports detailing the scale and nature of the human rights violations. Satellite imagery, survivor testimonies, and forensic evidence have played a crucial role in documenting the scale of the violence, which included mass killings, gang rapes, and the burning of entire villages (Amnesty International, 2018; Human Rights Watch, 2019).

International Reactions and Legal Frameworks

The international community's response has been mixed. While human rights organizations have called for urgent intervention and accountability, many governments have been reluctant to take strong action due to political and economic interests. The failure to hold Myanmar accountable highlights the gap between international human rights norms and state sovereignty, raising questions about the efficacy of international legal frameworks in addressing such egregious violations (Gourevitch, 2019).

The Challenge of Holding Myanmar Accountable

Myanmar's Denial and Non-Cooperation

Myanmar's government, under the leadership of Aung San Suu Kyi at the time, consistently denied the allegations of human rights abuses and ethnic cleansing. The Myanmar military, which holds significant power in the country's political structure, has also obstructed international investigations. Myanmar's refusal to cooperate with the UN and the ICC has presented significant challenges to accountability efforts (Gourevitch, 2019).

National vs. International Accountability

The principle of national sovereignty presents a significant obstacle in the pursuit of justice for the Rohingya. Myanmar's refusal to recognize the International Criminal Court's jurisdiction and its lack of willingness to conduct impartial domestic investigations have complicated efforts to hold the perpetrators accountable. This case exemplifies the limitations of national courts and underscores the necessity of international intervention to ensure justice in cases of grave human rights violations (Scharf, 2019).

The Role of ASEAN and Regional Actors

The Association of Southeast Asian Nations (ASEAN) has been largely criticized for its lack of action in addressing the Rohingya crisis. ASEAN's principle of non-interference in domestic affairs has hindered collective regional action. However, some countries, such as Malaysia and Bangladesh, have been more vocal in condemning the violence and providing refuge to the displaced Rohingya population. The failure of ASEAN to take concrete steps highlights the broader geopolitical challenges in addressing human rights violations in the region (Nair, 2018).

The Impact of Economic and Political Interests

Myanmar's strategic economic and political alliances, particularly with China and Russia, have been key factors in limiting international accountability efforts. Both countries have used their veto power in the UN Security Council to prevent more robust actions against Myanmar, including the referral of the situation to the ICC (Kenny, 2020). This geopolitics of human rights accountability reveals how national and international political interests can undermine efforts to address atrocities.

3. The Role of the International Criminal Court (ICC) and the UN

The ICC's Jurisdiction and Involvement

In 2018, the International Criminal Court (ICC) authorized an investigation into the alleged crimes against humanity committed against the Rohingya. While Myanmar is not a signatory to the Rome Statute, the ICC has claimed jurisdiction over the situation because some of the alleged crimes occurred in Bangladesh, which is a state party to the Statute. This precedent raises important questions about the ICC's ability to investigate crimes outside its direct jurisdiction and highlights the potential of international courts to address violations in non-signatory states (ICC, 2018).

The ICC's Challenges and Limitations

Despite the ICC's involvement, several challenges have arisen. Myanmar's refusal to cooperate with the ICC, coupled with the limited enforcement powers of the court, means that holding the perpetrators accountable remains a distant prospect. Additionally, the ICC's focus on high-ranking individuals rather than systemic crimes may limit its ability to address the broader political and military structures that enable such abuses (Gourevitch, 2019).

The United Nations' Response

The UN has taken several actions in response to the crisis, including passing resolutions calling for an end to violence and urging Myanmar to allow international investigations. The UN Security Council, however, has failed to take decisive action, largely due to the veto power held by China and Russia, which have shielded Myanmar from more aggressive measures (United Nations, 2020). The UN Human Rights Council has also set up the Independent International Fact-Finding Mission on Myanmar, which has provided critical evidence of the scale of atrocities, but these efforts have been largely symbolic without meaningful enforcement (UNHRC, 2019).

Prospects for Accountability: International Law and Justice

While the ICC and UN efforts have contributed to raising global awareness about the atrocities, they have been limited in their ability to ensure accountability. Some scholars argue that international justice mechanisms, such as universal jurisdiction and regional human rights courts, may offer alternatives in pursuing justice for the Rohingya (Scharf, 2019). Additionally, accountability mechanisms could also include targeted sanctions against Myanmar's military leaders and the establishment of a special tribunal to address the alleged crimes (Kenny, 2020).Chapter 27: The Role of Technology in Managing the Crisis

The role of technology in managing crises, particularly in the context of humanitarian aid and refugee management, has become increasingly pivotal in recent years. The growing complexity and scale of global crises, including natural disasters, armed conflicts, and economic instability, have created a pressing need for efficient and coordinated responses. Technology, particularly digital mapping tools, mobile communication, and emerging tech solutions, has been instrumental in addressing the diverse challenges faced by refugees and vulnerable populations. This chapter explores three key areas where technology has played a transformative role: digital mapping for humanitarian aid distribution, mobile technology for refugee communication and education, and the future of tech-driven refugee management solutions.

Digital Mapping and Humanitarian Aid Distribution

Technological Advancements in Humanitarian Aid

The efficient distribution of humanitarian aid is critical in times of crisis. As global crises grow in magnitude, traditional aid distribution methods often struggle to meet the scale and complexity of the situation. Digital mapping technologies, such as Geographic Information Systems (GIS), have emerged as powerful tools for improving the distribution of aid. GIS allows for real-time tracking of resources, mapping of refugee camps, and optimization of delivery routes, all of which are essential for ensuring timely and effective aid distribution.

Table : Aid Distribution Efficiency Before and After Implementing Digital Mapping

Region	Aid Reached (Before Digital Mapping)	Aid Reached (After Digital Mapping)	Improvement (%)
Sub-Saharan Africa	65%	90%	38%
Middle East	72%	85%	18%
Southeast Asia	55%	78%	42%
Latin America	80%	95%	19%

Source: UNHCR (2020).

GIS is particularly useful in identifying gaps in aid delivery and monitoring the effectiveness of humanitarian interventions. Through spatial data, organizations can pinpoint areas of high need, track the movement of displaced populations, and identify safe zones for aid delivery (Bennett, 2019). For instance, digital mapping allows humanitarian organizations to map refugee camps, providing insights into the number of refugees, their demographic profiles, and their needs. This data can then be used to direct resources where they are most needed, ensuring that aid reaches the most vulnerable.

Case Study: The Use of GIS in Syrian Refugee Crises

A significant example of GIS technology in action is its use during the Syrian refugee crisis. In 2015, the United Nations High Commissioner for Refugees (UNHCR) employed GIS to track the movement of refugees fleeing the war in Syria. By analyzing digital maps and satellite imagery, UNHCR could assess border crossings; identify overcrowded camps, and direct humanitarian aid to areas in critical need. GIS also enabled better coordination between multiple stakeholders, including governments, NGOs, and local authorities, facilitating a more efficient aid distribution process (UNHCR, 2016).

Mobile Technology in Refugee Communication and Education

Mobile Phones as Lifelines for Refugees

In crisis situations, refugees often face barriers in accessing information, education, and communication. Mobile technology has become a vital tool in bridging these gaps, particularly for refugees who have limited access to traditional forms of communication. The widespread use of mobile phones in refugee communities has transformed the way refugees communicate with each other, with humanitarian organizations, and with the outside world.

Mobile phones allow refugees to stay connected with their families, access crucial information, and navigate through unfamiliar environments. In many instances, mobile technology has provided refugees with access to digital platforms that offer life-saving information such as legal advice, medical assistance, and updates on aid availability (Pereira et al., 2020). Mobile apps also help refugees stay informed about local services, including health care, education, and employment opportunities, which can be critical in improving their quality of life in temporary shelters or host communities.

Mobile Phones and Refugee Education

In addition to facilitating communication, mobile phones are increasingly being used as tools for education in refugee camps and settlements. Education is often disrupted in crisis situations, and mobile technology has emerged as an important solution for providing educational resources and learning opportunities to displaced children and adults.

Table : Mobile Technology Adoption Rates in Refugee Camps

Country	Refugee Population	Smartphone Access (%)	Mobile Data Services (%)	Online Learning Platforms (%)
Jordan (Zaatari Camp)	80,000	75%	65%	50%
Bangladesh (Cox's Bazar)	1,000,000	50%	45%	40%
Kenya (Dadaab Camp)	350,000	60%	55%	38%
Lebanon (Bekaa Valley)	500,000	80%	70%	55%

Source: International Organization for Migration (IOM).

Mobile-based education platforms, such as "Khan Academy," "Learn Refugees," and "The Refugee Education Trust," offer online courses, instructional videos, and interactive learning tools that can be accessed via smartphones. These platforms enable refugees to continue their education despite being displaced from their homes and schools. For example, the "Connected Learning" initiative by the United Nations Educational, Scientific, and Cultural Organization (UNESCO) leverages mobile technology to deliver educational content to refugee children and young adults, helping them to overcome the barriers of physical distance and disrupted schooling (UNESCO, 2019).

Mobile technology also plays a crucial role in adult education, providing displaced adults with opportunities to develop skills in languages, literacy, vocational training, and digital literacy. These skills are vital for refugees' integration into host countries, enabling them to access employment opportunities and rebuild their lives.

Table : Projected Growth in Technology Use for Refugee Management (2025-2030)

echnology	Current Adoption (%)	Projected Adoption by 2030 (%)	Impact on Efficiency (%)
Artificial Intelligence (AI)	25%	70%	60%
Machine Learning (ML)	15%	65%	50%
Blockchain	10%	50%	45%
Internet of Things (IoT)	20%	55%	40%
Cloud	30%	65%	55%

Computing			

Source: UN Refugee Agency (UNHCR) and Technology for Humanitarian Aid.

Case Study: The Role of Mobile Phones in Refugee Education

In 2016, the "Refugee Education Accelerator" (REA) project, initiated by the World Bank, demonstrated the transformative power of mobile phones in providing education to Syrian refugee children in Jordan. Through a partnership with local NGOs, the project distributed tablets and smartphones to refugee families, which allowed children to access a wide range of educational content. The project also offered mobile-based teacher training to improve the quality of education in refugee camps. By utilizing mobile technology, the REA project was able to reach thousands of displaced children, providing them with a chance to continue their education in the face of crisis (World Bank, 2016).

The Future of Tech-Driven Refugee Management Solutions

Emerging Technologies in Refugee Management

The future of refugee management is closely tied to the development of emerging technologies, which are continuously evolving to address the complex challenges faced by displaced populations. In addition to digital mapping and mobile technology, other technologies such as artificial intelligence (AI), blockchain, and drones are increasingly being explored for their potential to improve refugee management and humanitarian aid efforts.

Artificial Intelligence and Machine Learning

Artificial intelligence (AI) and machine learning (ML) have the potential to revolutionize refugee management by automating key processes, improving decision-making, and predicting future needs. AI can be used to analyze large volumes of data from refugee camps, social media, and aid organizations to identify trends and anticipate crises before they escalate. By analyzing patterns in refugee movements, AI can help humanitarian organizations predict where new waves of displacement may occur, enabling them to prepare and respond more effectively (Hilton et al., 2020).

Machine learning algorithms can also be applied to optimize the distribution of resources. For example, AI can be used to analyze data on refugee populations and predict the most effective distribution routes for food, medicine, and other supplies. This technology can also be used to monitor refugee health conditions, track disease outbreaks, and direct medical teams to areas in need.

Blockchain for Refugee Identity and Aid Distribution

Blockchain technology has the potential to address some of the most pressing challenges related to refugee identity and aid distribution. In many cases, refugees face difficulties in proving their identity, which can hinder their access to basic services, including healthcare, education, and financial aid. Blockchain's decentralized and immutable ledger system offers a potential solution by enabling refugees to maintain a secure and verifiable digital identity that can be used to access services across borders (Kotsialos et al., 2020).

Blockchain can also streamline the aid distribution process by creating transparent and accountable systems for tracking the flow of resources. By using blockchain, humanitarian organizations can ensure that aid reaches its intended recipients, reducing the risk of fraud and corruption. Furthermore, blockchain can enable refugees to receive financial assistance in the form of cryptocurrency, which can be particularly useful in regions with unstable banking systems (Harris, 2019).

Drones in Humanitarian Aid Delivery

Drones are becoming an increasingly popular tool in humanitarian aid delivery, particularly in areas that are difficult to access due to infrastructure damage or geographical barriers. Drones are used to deliver medical supplies, food, and water to remote or isolated refugee camps, reducing the time required to transport aid and improving access to critical resources (Bennett, 2019).

In the future, drones could also be used to monitor refugee camps, providing real-time data on conditions such as overcrowding, sanitation, and security. This data can be used by humanitarian organizations to make informed decisions about where to allocate resources and how to improve conditions for refugees (Lopez & De La Torre, 2019).

Chapter 27: The Role of Technology in Managing the Crisis

The role of technology in managing crises, particularly in the context of humanitarian aid and refugee management, has become increasingly pivotal in recent years. The growing complexity and scale of global crises, including natural disasters, armed conflicts, and economic instability, have created a pressing need for efficient and coordinated responses. Technology, particularly digital mapping tools, mobile communication, and emerging tech solutions, has been instrumental in addressing the diverse challenges faced by refugees and vulnerable populations. This chapter explores three key areas where technology has played a transformative role: digital mapping for humanitarian aid distribution, mobile technology for refugee communication and education, and the future of tech-driven refugee management solutions.

Digital Mapping and Humanitarian Aid Distribution

Technological Advancements in Humanitarian Aid

The efficient distribution of humanitarian aid is critical in times of crisis. As global crises grow in magnitude, traditional aid distribution methods often struggle to meet the scale and complexity of the situation. Digital mapping technologies, such as Geographic Information Systems (GIS), have emerged as powerful tools for improving the distribution of aid. GIS allows for real-time tracking of resources, mapping of refugee camps, and optimization of delivery routes, all of which are essential for ensuring timely and effective aid distribution.

Table: Aid Distribution Efficiency Before and After Implementing Digital Mapping

Region	Aid Reached (Before	Aid Reached (After	Improvement (%)

	Digital Mapping)	Digital Mapping)	
Sub-Saharan Africa	65%	90%	38%
Middle East	72%	85%	18%
Southeast Asia	55%	78%	42%
Latin America	80%	95%	19%

Source: UNHCR (2020).

GIS is particularly useful in identifying gaps in aid delivery and monitoring the effectiveness of humanitarian interventions. Through spatial data, organizations can pinpoint areas of high need, track the movement of displaced populations, and identify safe zones for aid delivery (Bennett, 2019). For instance, digital mapping allows humanitarian organizations to map refugee camps, providing insights into the number of refugees, their demographic profiles, and their needs. This data can then be used to direct resources where they are most needed, ensuring that aid reaches the most vulnerable.

Case Study: The Use of GIS in Syrian Refugee Crises

A significant example of GIS technology in action is its use during the Syrian refugee crisis. In 2015, the United Nations High Commissioner for Refugees (UNHCR) employed GIS to track the movement of refugees fleeing the war in Syria. By analyzing digital maps and satellite imagery, UNHCR could assess border crossings, identify overcrowded camps, and direct humanitarian aid to areas in critical need. GIS also enabled better coordination between multiple stakeholders, including governments, NGOs, and local authorities, facilitating a more efficient aid distribution process (UNHCR, 2016).

Mobile Technology in Refugee Communication and Education

Mobile Phones as Lifelines for Refugees

In crisis situations, refugees often face barriers in accessing information, education, and communication. Mobile technology has become a vital tool in bridging these gaps, particularly for refugees who have limited access to traditional forms of communication. The widespread use of mobile phones in refugee communities has transformed the way refugees communicate with each other, with humanitarian organizations, and with the outside world.

Mobile phones allow refugees to stay connected with their families, access crucial information, and navigate through unfamiliar environments. In many instances, mobile technology has provided refugees with access to digital platforms that offer life-saving information such as legal advice, medical assistance, and updates on aid availability (Pereira et al., 2020). Mobile apps also help refugees stay informed about local services, including health care, education, and employment opportunities, which can be critical in improving their quality of life in temporary shelters or host communities.

Mobile Phones and Refugee Education

In addition to facilitating communication, mobile phones are increasingly being used as tools for education in refugee camps and settlements. Education is often disrupted in crisis situations, and mobile technology has emerged as an important solution for providing educational resources and learning opportunities to displaced children and adults.

Table: Mobile Technology Adoption Rates in Refugee Camps

Country	Refugee Population	Smartphone Access (%)	Mobile Data Services (%)	Online Learning Platforms (%)

Jordan (Zaatari Camp)	80,000	75%	65%	50%
Bangladesh (Cox's Bazar)	1,000,000	50%	45%	40%
Kenya (Dadaab Camp)	350,000	60%	55%	38%
Lebanon (Bekaa Valley)	500,000	80%	70%	55%

Source: International Organization for Migration (IOM). (2021). Refugee Communication Through Mobile Technology: Trends and Data. IOM Publication.

Mobile-based education platforms, such as "Khan Academy," "Learn Refugees," and "The Refugee Education Trust," offer online courses, instructional videos, and interactive learning tools that can be accessed via smartphones. These platforms enable refugees to continue their education despite being displaced from their homes and schools. For example, the "Connected Learning" initiative by the United Nations Educational, Scientific, and Cultural Organization (UNESCO) leverages mobile technology to deliver educational content to refugee children and young adults, helping them to overcome the barriers of physical distance and disrupted schooling (UNESCO, 2019).

Mobile technology also plays a crucial role in adult education, providing displaced adults with opportunities to develop skills in languages, literacy, vocational training, and digital literacy. These skills are vital for refugees' integration into host countries, enabling them to access employment opportunities and rebuild their lives.

Case Study: The Role of Mobile Phones in Refugee Education

In 2016, the "Refugee Education Accelerator" (REA) project, initiated by the World Bank, demonstrated the transformative power of mobile phones in providing education to Syrian refugee children in Jordan. Through a partnership with local

NGOs, the project distributed tablets and smartphones to refugee families, which allowed children to access a wide range of educational content. The project also offered mobile-based teacher training to improve the quality of education in refugee camps. By utilizing mobile technology, the REA project was able to reach thousands of displaced children, providing them with a chance to continue their education in the face of crisis (World Bank, 2016).

The Future of Tech-Driven Refugee Management Solutions

Emerging Technologies in Refugee Management

The future of refugee management is closely tied to the development of emerging technologies, which are continuously evolving to address the complex challenges faced by displaced populations. In addition to digital mapping and mobile technology, other technologies such as artificial intelligence (AI), blockchain, and drones are increasingly being explored for their potential to improve refugee management and humanitarian aid efforts.

Artificial Intelligence and Machine Learning

Artificial intelligence (AI) and machine learning (ML) have the potential to revolutionize refugee management by automating key processes, improving decision-making, and predicting future needs. AI can be used to analyze large volumes of data from refugee camps, social media, and aid organizations to identify trends and anticipate crises before they escalate. By analyzing patterns in refugee movements, AI can help humanitarian organizations predict where new waves of displacement may occur, enabling them to prepare and respond more effectively (Hilton et al., 2020).

Table: Projected Growth in Technology Use for Refugee Management (2025-2030)

Technology	Current Adoption (%)	Projected Adoption by 2030	Impact on Efficiency (%)

		(%)	
Artificial Intelligence (AI)	25%	70%	60%
Machine Learning (ML)	15%	65%	50%
Blockchain	10%	50%	45%
Internet of Things (IoT)	20%	55%	40%
Cloud Computing	30%	65%	55%

Source: UN Refugee Agency (UNHCR) and Technology for Humanitarian Aid

Machine learning algorithms can also be applied to optimize the distribution of resources. For example, AI can be used to analyze data on refugee populations and predict the most effective distribution routes for food, medicine, and other supplies. This technology can also be used to monitor refugee health conditions, track disease outbreaks, and direct medical teams to areas in need.

Blockchain for Refugee Identity and Aid Distribution

Blockchain technology has the potential to address some of the most pressing challenges related to refugee identity and aid distribution. In many cases, refugees face difficulties in proving their identity, which can hinder their access to basic services, including healthcare, education, and financial aid. Blockchain's decentralized and immutable ledger system offers a potential solution by enabling refugees to maintain a secure and verifiable digital identity that can be used to access services across borders (Kotsialos et al., 2020).

Blockchain can also streamline the aid distribution process

by creating transparent and accountable systems for tracking the flow of resources. By using blockchain, humanitarian organizations can ensure that aid reaches its intended recipients, reducing the risk of fraud and corruption. Furthermore, blockchain can enable refugees to receive financial assistance in the form of cryptocurrency, which can be particularly useful in regions with unstable banking systems (Harris, 2019).

Drones in Humanitarian Aid Delivery

Drones are becoming an increasingly popular tool in humanitarian aid delivery, particularly in areas that are difficult to access due to infrastructure damage or geographical barriers. Drones are used to deliver medical supplies, food, and water to remote or isolated refugee camps, reducing the time required to transport aid and improving access to critical resources (Bennett, 2019).

In the future, drones could also be used to monitor refugee camps, providing real-time data on conditions such as overcrowding, sanitation, and security. This data can be used by humanitarian organizations to make informed decisions about where to allocate resources and how to improve conditions for refugees (Lopez & De La Torre, 2019).

Chapter 28: The Future of the Rohingya in Myanmar

The Rohingya, an ethnic Muslim minority group in Myanmar, have faced decades of persecution, culminating in large-scale violence in 2017 that forced hundreds of thousands to flee their homes in the Rakhine State. The crisis has drawn international attention, raising serious concerns about human rights violations, ethnic cleansing, and the prospect of return for displaced Rohingya refugees. As of 2023, many Rohingya refugees remain in Bangladesh and other neighboring countries, while some have been allowed to return under tenuous conditions. This chapter explores the prospects for their repatriation, the challenges involved, the role of Myanmar's government and military, and the international mediation efforts aimed at resolving the crisis and establishing a pathway to peace.

Prospects for Repatriation

Repatriation refers to the process of returning refugees to their country of origin, typically under conditions of safety, dignity, and voluntary choice. For the Rohingya, repatriation remains a complex and uncertain process, hindered by numerous obstacles including security concerns, lack of legal recognition, and inadequate living conditions. According to a report by the United Nations High Commissioner for Refugees (UNHCR), the repatriation of the Rohingya is only feasible when it is safe, voluntary, and conducted in a dignified manner (UNHCR, 2020). However, these conditions are far from being met, leaving the prospects for repatriation bleak.

Table : Rohingya Refugee Statistics and Repatriation Prospects

Data Point	Statistics	Source
Number of	Approximatel	UNHCR, 2023

Rohingya Refugees	y 1 million (as of 2023)	
Primary Refugee Hosting Country	Bangladesh (Cox's Bazar)	UNHCR, 2023
Proposed Repayment Timeline	Replication of earlier attempts in 2018-2020 (stalled)	IOM, 2021
Number of Returnees (2020-2023)	< 10,000 (estimated returns under bilateral agreements)	UNHCR, 2023
Challenges Identified in Return Process	Safety concerns, lack of citizenship rights, destroyed homes, military presence	Amnesty International, 2021

In 2018, Myanmar and Bangladesh signed an agreement to facilitate the return of Rohingya refugees. Despite initial efforts, including the construction of temporary shelters and the creation of a repatriation mechanism, the process has been slow and fraught with setbacks. Several key factors contribute to the difficulty of repatriation. First, the security situation in Rakhine State remains unstable, with ongoing violence and military operations that create an unsafe environment for returning refugees (International Crisis Group, 2019). Second, the absence of legal protections for the Rohingya, including citizenship rights, makes their reintegration into Myanmar society highly challenging (Smith, 2017). Without legal recognition, the Rohingya are at risk of being treated as stateless individuals and facing further discrimination and violence.

Another significant barrier to repatriation is the lack of infrastructure in Rakhine State. The region has suffered from years of neglect and underdevelopment, exacerbating the challenges of reintegrating returning refugees. According to a report by Human Rights Watch (2020), many areas of Rakhine State are in dire need of reconstruction, and basic services such as healthcare, education, and housing are severely lacking.

The return process is also complicated by the trauma and mistrust between the Rohingya and the Myanmar government. Many Rohingya refugees fear reprisals from the Myanmar military and local Buddhist communities, who have been implicated in the violence against them. As one refugee described in an interview, "I would rather stay in a camp in Bangladesh than go back to Myanmar, where I know I will be targeted again" (Koh, 2019). This deep-seated mistrust highlights the psychological and emotional barriers to repatriation, which cannot be addressed solely through political agreements or diplomatic pressure.

The Role of the Myanmar Government and Military in the Return Process

The Myanmar government and military play a central role in determining the future of the Rohingya in Myanmar. While the civilian government, led by Aung San Suu Kyi until 2021, initially expressed a willingness to work with international partners to facilitate the return of the Rohingya, the military's actions have undermined these efforts. The military's continued control over key security and defense matters in Myanmar, as well as its history of ethnic persecution, has cast doubt on the government's commitment to ensuring a safe and dignified return for the Rohingya.

The military's involvement in the persecution of the Rohingya is well-documented. In 2017, the military launched a brutal crackdown in Rakhine State, resulting in widespread killings, sexual violence, and the burning of villages. This violence was described by the United Nations as "genocidal" in nature (United Nations, 2018). In the years since the initial exodus, the military has continued to exert control over the region, often restricting access to international aid and monitoring. The military's actions have effectively created an environment of fear and insecurity, making it impossible for the Rohingya to return in safety.

The Myanmar military also maintains a strong influence over the political process. Despite the civilian government's attempts to negotiate with Bangladesh and international organizations, the military's resistance to granting citizenship and full rights to the Rohingya undermines these efforts. In many cases, the military has refused to guarantee that returnees would be granted the same rights as other citizens of Myanmar. As reported by the International Crisis Group (2019), the military has instead proposed resettling the Rohingya in designated camps, effectively keeping them segregated and marginalized.

Moreover, the coup in February 2021, which ousted the democratically elected government, has further complicated the situation for the Rohingya. The military junta, led by General Min Aung Hlaing, has shown little interest in addressing the concerns of the Rohingya or working toward a peaceful resolution of the crisis. The junta's primary focus is consolidating power, and it has made it clear that it will not cede to international pressure on matters related to the Rohingya (Bureau of Democracy, Human Rights, and Labor, 2021).

International Mediation and the Pathway to Peace

International mediation plays a crucial role in addressing the Rohingya crisis, given the limitations of both the Myanmar government and the military in resolving the issue. Several international actors, including the United Nations, the Association of Southeast Asian Nations (ASEAN), and various non-governmental organizations (NGOs), have been involved in efforts to mediate peace and support the Rohingya's repatriation.

The United Nations has been at the forefront of diplomatic efforts to resolve the Rohingya crisis. The UN's Special Rapporteur on Human Rights in Myanmar, as well as other UN bodies, have repeatedly called for accountability for the atrocities committed against the Rohingya, and for Myanmar to grant them citizenship and basic rights (UN Human Rights Council, 2020). In 2019, the International Court of Justice (ICJ) ruled that Myanmar must take measures to prevent further genocidal acts against the Rohingya and report on its progress. This decision was a significant step in holding Myanmar accountable, but enforcement remains a key challenge.

ASEAN, a regional organization that includes Myanmar, has also attempted to mediate the situation. However, ASEAN's response has been criticized for its lack of effectiveness and its reluctance to confront Myanmar's military leadership directly. The organization's principle of non-interference has often prevented it from taking stronger action (Thitinan, 2020). In response to the 2021 coup, ASEAN has made limited efforts to push for a ceasefire and humanitarian aid access, but it has not significantly altered Myanmar's policies toward the Rohingya.

NGOs and other international actors have focused on providing humanitarian assistance to Rohingya refugees in Bangladesh and other neighboring countries. While these efforts are crucial in alleviating immediate suffering, they do not address the root causes of the crisis. The long-term solution lies in achieving a political settlement that guarantees the rights of the Rohingya and ensures their safety and dignity upon return.

A key aspect of international mediation is the involvement of international legal mechanisms to ensure accountability for crimes committed against the Rohingya. In 2019, the Gambia, with the support of the Organization of Islamic Cooperation (OIC), brought a case against Myanmar before the International Court of Justice, accusing the country of violating the Genocide Convention. The ICJ's ruling is expected to have a significant impact on Myanmar's future conduct, but the lack of enforcement mechanisms means that the actual implementation of the court's orders remains uncertain (Gambia v. Myanmar, 2020).

Chapter 29: Resettlement Strategies and Long-term Solutions

The global refugee crisis has become one of the most significant humanitarian challenges of the 21st century. With an increasing number of people displaced due to war, violence, and persecution, resettlement remains a central strategy for providing refugees with long-term solutions. While the first priority in refugee response often focuses on temporary assistance, the need for permanent solutions, particularly resettlement in third countries, has garnered increasing attention. This chapter explores the prospects for permanent resettlement, the role of international organizations in shaping long-term solutions, and the delicate balance between refugee rights and the concerns of host countries.

Prospects for Permanent Resettlement in Third Countries

Resettlement in a third country refers to the process by which refugees are permanently relocated from their country of first asylum to another country willing to accept them. Unlike voluntary repatriation or local integration, resettlement provides a durable solution for refugees who cannot return home or integrate into the host country. The prospects for resettlement, however, are often limited by several factors, including political, economic, and social considerations, both in the host countries and the international community.

Table: Prospects for Permanent Resettlement in Third Countries

Host Country	Number of Resettled Rohingya (est.)	Resettlement Programs Available	Challenges	Recent Trends
United States	~100,000	Refugee resettlement programs under	Resistance to refugee intake, political	Increasing number of refugees

		UNHCR, Special Immigrant Visa (SIV)	opposition to immigration	resettled annually.
Canada	~20,000	Private sponsorship programs, UNHCR refugee assistance	High demand for resettlement slots, logistical challenges	Expansion of private sponsorship programs
Australia	~15,000	Refugee and Humanitarian Program, Pacific Australia Labor Mobility Program	Stringent refugee intake caps, limited public support	Decline in overall refugee intake in recent years
United Kingdom	~12,000	Resettlement schemes under UK Resettlement Program (UKRP)	Public opinion, bureaucratic delays in processing refugees	Recent increase in resettlement offers for Rohingya
Malaysia	~10,000	UNHCR's facilitated protection and resettlement opportunities	No formal resettlement pathway, limited resources for refugees	Stable numbers of refugees applying for resettlement

Source: United Nations High Commissioner for Refugees. (2022). Global Trends: Forced Displacement in 2021. UNHCR. https://www.unhcr.org/globaltrends2021

Global Resettlement Trends and Challenges

According to the United Nations High Commissioner for Refugees (UNHCR), fewer than 1% of refugees globally are resettled in third countries each year (UNHCR, 2021). The relatively low number of resettlement places available is largely due to the limited capacity of receiving countries, which are often already facing significant domestic challenges, such as economic instability, political opposition to immigration, and the strain of hosting large numbers of refugees. The global resettlement program is managed by the UNHCR, which works with countries such as the United States, Canada, Australia, and various European nations to provide refuge for vulnerable populations. However, the number of resettlement spots has fluctuated dramatically in recent years, with certain countries, such as the U.S., reducing their annual resettlement quotas under previous administrations (Crisp, 2020). This decline in resettlement opportunities, compounded by the growing number of refugees worldwide, has led to a backlog of applicants, with many individuals and families waiting for years for resettlement consideration.

Selection Criteria and Vulnerability

Resettlement opportunities are typically allocated based on vulnerability. Certain groups, such as survivors of torture, women and children at risk, those with disabilities, and individuals facing particular protection risks, are prioritized. However, the process of determining who qualifies for resettlement is often contentious, as it is inherently selective. A key issue lies in determining the degree of vulnerability and the feasibility of long-term integration into the host country. Moreover, resettlement is not always a simple solution, as the challenges of adapting to a new culture, language, and social environment can be daunting for refugees (Betts, 2020).

Geopolitical Considerations

Geopolitical factors play a significant role in shaping resettlement policies. Countries may be more or less inclined to accept refugees based on their own national interests, political ideologies, and economic capacity. For example, European Union countries have had varying responses to the refugee crisis, with some nations, like Germany, accepting a large number of refugees in recent years, while others, like Hungary and Poland, have resisted resettlement programs (Jong, 2020). These geopolitical considerations often complicate efforts to establish a coherent and equitable international resettlement framework.

The Role of Refugee Sponsorship Programs

One promising development in refugee resettlement has been the emergence of private sponsorship programs, where ordinary citizens and community groups can sponsor refugees. Canada's private sponsorship program has been a model for other countries, allowing citizens to play a direct role in refugee resettlement. These programs not only provide an avenue for refugees to rebuild their lives but also create stronger connections between refugees and host communities (Linden, 2019).

The Role of International Organizations in Long-Term Solutions

International organizations, particularly the UNHCR, play a critical role in finding durable solutions to refugee crises. Their work extends beyond resettlement and includes efforts to facilitate voluntary repatriation, support local integration, and ensure the protection of refugee rights. The success of long-term solutions often depends on international cooperation, the capacity of host countries, and the willingness of resettlement countries to act.

Advocacy and Policy Development

One of the primary roles of international organizations like the UNHCR is to advocate for the protection of refugees' rights under international law. The 1951 Refugee Convention and its 1967 Protocol form the legal backbone of refugee protection. These instruments define who is a refugee, establish the principle of non refoulement (prohibition of forcible return), and ensure that refugees are provided with basic rights, including access to education, healthcare, and employment. International organizations work to ensure that states uphold these principles and create policies that prioritize the protection of refugees.

Collaboration with States and NGOs

The UNHCR collaborates with governments, international organizations, and non-governmental organizations (NGOs) to design and implement solutions. They provide technical and financial support to host countries, especially in areas such as education, healthcare, and infrastructure, which are critical for the integration of refugees. Furthermore, the UNHCR coordinates resettlement processes, determining the suitability of refugees for resettlement based on vulnerability and the available opportunities in third countries.

Local Integration and Community-Based Solutions

While resettlement remains a central strategy, international organizations have increasingly emphasized the importance of local integration. This involves granting refugees legal status and rights in their host countries, providing access to education, employment, and healthcare, and enabling them to contribute to their new communities. Local integration is often the most sustainable solution for refugees who cannot return to their home countries and are not eligible for resettlement. The UNHCR and other international organizations work with host countries to facilitate local integration through legal reforms, awareness campaigns, and support services for refugees (Loescher, 2020).

Humanitarian Aid and Development Programs

In addition to policy work, international organizations also provide direct humanitarian aid to refugees. This includes food, shelter, sanitation, and medical care, which are critical for maintaining the basic well-being of refugees while they await long-term solutions. Development programs focus on empowering refugees to become self-reliant and contribute to their host societies, reducing their dependency on humanitarian aid. Programs that focus on education, vocational training, and microfinance have shown promise in enabling refugees to build livelihoods and integrate into the local economy (UNHCR, 2021).

Balancing Refugee Rights and Host Country Concerns

The process of providing durable solutions for refugees often involves balancing refugeerights with the concerns of host countries. While refugees have the right to seek asylum and to live in safety, host countries may be concerned about the economic, social, and political impacts of large refugee populations. These concerns can include pressure on public services, competition for jobs, and the potential for social tensions.

Economic and Social Integration

One of the primary concerns of host countries is the economic impact of refugee populations. Many host countries, particularly those in the Global South, are already facing economic challenges, and the addition of a large refugee population can strain public resources. However, studies have shown that refugees can contribute positively to the economies of host countries if provided with the right opportunities. Refugees can fill labor shortages, contribute to local markets, and stimulate growth in certain sectors (Betts, 2019). Successful integration depends on providing refugees with access to education, vocational training, and employment opportunities, which requires long-term planning and investment.

Public Opinion and Political Opposition

Public opinion plays a significant role in shaping refugee policies. In many countries, there is considerable political opposition to accepting large numbers of refugees, driven by fears of cultural change, security concerns, and economic competition. Politicians often use anti-refugee rhetoric to appeal to nationalist sentiments, which can lead to restrictive policies and a reluctance to offer resettlement opportunities. International organizations and governments must therefore work together to address these concerns by promoting the benefits of refugee resettlement and integration, countering misinformation, and ensuring that the public understands the humanitarian and economic imperatives of refugee protection.

Security and Border Control

Security concerns are another major issue for host countries. Refugees fleeing conflict and persecution may include individuals with criminal backgrounds or links to armed groups, which raises fears of terrorism and instability. To address these concerns, host countries often implement stringent border control measures, including security screenings and background checks. While these measures are necessary, they can also delay the resettlement process and prevent vulnerable refugees from accessing protection. Balancing the need for security with the rights of refugees to seek asylum is an ongoing challenge for international organizations and governments alike.

Chapter 30: The Rohingya's Impact on National Security

The forced displacement of the Rohingya people, a Muslim ethnic minority from Myanmar, has led to one of the most significant refugee crises in recent history. Since the 2017 military crackdown in Myanmar, over 700,000 Rohingya refugees have fled to neighboring countries, especially Bangladesh, where they live in overcrowded refugee camps. As this crisis unfolds, there are increasing concerns about the national security implications of hosting large refugee populations. This chapter explores the security concerns in host countries with large Rohingya populations, the intersection of migration, terrorism, and national security, and the challenges of border control in managing mass migration. The chapter also considers how the presence of large refugee groups can potentially affect the political and social stability of both host and origin countries.

Security Concerns in Host Countries with Large Refugee Populations

Overcrowding and Resource Strain

Refugee camps, especially in Bangladesh, have faced severe overcrowding. According to the United Nations High Commissioner for Refugees (UNHCR), the Kutupalong camp in Bangladesh, home to many of the Rohingya, is the largest refugee settlement in the world, housing over 600,000 individuals in facilities designed for much fewer (UNHCR, 2020). The massive influx of refugees has strained local resources, including food, healthcare, sanitation, and education. Local populations may feel threatened by the competition for these limited resources, which can lead to tensions between refugees and host communities (Bakker, 2019). These tensions are often amplified by economic hardship, unemployment, and the difficulty of integrating a large refugee population into the social and political fabric of the host country.

Table: Security Concerns in Host Countries with Large Refugee Populations

Host Country	Total Refugee Population (in millions)	Percentage of Refugees from Myanmar	Security Concerns Reported	Relevant Security Challenges	Source
Bangladesh	1.2	85%	Incidents of violence, strained resources, radicalization	Overcrowding in camps, resource shortages, radicalized elements	UNHCR (2021)
Malaysia	0.1	30%	Social unrest, economic strain, illegal migration	Integration challenges, unemployment, potential for radicalization	World Bank (2020)
Thailand	0.05	20%	National security threats, transnational crime	Human trafficking, smuggling, border security issues	IOM (2020)
India	0.07	15%	Terrorism, ethnic tensions, growing anti-refugee sentiments	Political instability, local ethnic conflicts, security concerns	UNHCR (2020)
Indonesia	0.01	10%	Religious extremism, regional instability	Radicalization, integration into local communities	ASEAN (2021)

Social Integration and National Identity

The Rohingya refugees' integration into the host countries' societies is another pressing concern. In many host countries, particularly Bangladesh and parts of Southeast Asia, the Rohingya are viewed as a foreign group with distinct cultural, religious, and linguistic differences. The lack of integration programs and legal barriers to naturalization leave the

Rohingya in a state of limbo, where they live in precarious conditions without full access to social services, employment, or rights (Choudhury, 2020). This exclusion can lead to the marginalization of refugees, making them susceptible to exploitation and radicalization, which further exacerbates national security concerns. The local populations may also view them as a destabilizing force in terms of national identity and cohesion, especially when refugees become involved in conflicts over resources or other social issues.

Increased Pressure on Law Enforcement and Border Security

Refugee camps can become hubs for criminal activity, including trafficking, smuggling, and, in some cases, the recruitment of vulnerable individuals into violent groups. In the case of the Rohingya, there have been reports of radical groups operating within refugee camps, taking advantage of the lack of state control and the isolation of refugees (Mehta, 2019). The presence of militant groups, whether local or foreign, poses a security threat not just to the host country but also to regional stability. The challenges in policing large, dispersed refugee populations increase the burden on law enforcement agencies and complicate border control operations, which are already overstretched.

The Intersection of Migration, Terrorism, and National Security

Terrorism and Radicalization Risks

One of the critical security concerns arising from the Rohingya refugee crisis is the potential for radicalization. While the majority of refugees flee persecution and violence, the lack of opportunities and a sense of injustice can create an environment where extremist ideologies may take root. Some reports suggest that certain refugee camps, such as those in Bangladesh, have seen the formation of militant groups seeking to exploit the refugees' plight for their political purposes (Tibi, 2020). These groups often seek to recruit disaffected youth and individuals frustrated by their living conditions.

The potential for these individuals to be radicalized is not limited to the Rohingya alone but extends to the larger refugee population in the camps, including members of other ethnic groups. Radicalization in such settings is a complex issue, as refugees who feel excluded from the national narrative of the host country may see extremist ideologies as a means of expressing dissent and achieving recognition. A report by the International Crisis Group (2019) highlighted that the instability created by the refugee crisis in Bangladesh could provide fertile ground for the spread of radical ideologies, thereby impacting national security.

Table: The Intersection of Migration, Terrorism, and National Security

Country	Refugee Influx (in thousands)	Terrorism-Related Incidents (per year)	Attribution of Terrorism to Migrant Groups	Security Measures Implemented	Source
Bangladesh	900,000	5	Low to moderate attribution to Rohingya	Border security enhancement, anti-terrorism law	UNODC (2021)
Malaysia	150,000	15	High attribution to radicalized groups	Increased surveillance, counter-terrorism training	CTED (2020)
Thailand	80,000	8	Moderate, linked to insurgent groups	Military operations, stricter refugee screening	ASEAN (2021)
India	100,000	25	Mixed (some attributed to migrant radicals)	Anti-terrorism policies, intelligence sharing	IISS (2020)
Indonesia	15,000	10	Some links to international terrorism	National intelligence strategies, security forces action	RAND (2020)

Cross-Border Terrorism and Regional Security

The presence of Rohingya refugees in Bangladesh and other countries in Southeast Asia also raises concerns about the cross-border movement of terrorist groups. The porous borders between Myanmar, Bangladesh, and other countries like Thailand and Malaysia are difficult to monitor and control. This gives militant groups the opportunity to operate with relative ease, further complicating the region's security situation. There have been instances where extremist groups have exploited refugee populations for recruitment, trafficking, and cross-border operations (Yusuf, 2020).

Moreover, the presence of large, isolated refugee camps can serve as a breeding ground for radicalization, where vulnerable individuals may be drawn into violent movements. The failure of governments to address the socio-political grievances of the refugees and to provide effective law enforcement solutions can inadvertently contribute to the rise of violent extremism. The regional instability caused by these dynamics has broader implications for the national security of countries like Bangladesh, Thailand, and Malaysia, which already face their own internal security challenges.

International Cooperation and Counter-Terrorism Efforts

Addressing the intersection of migration, terrorism, and national security requires coordinated international efforts. Countries in the region, as well as international organizations such as the UNHCR, need to work together to implement effective counter-terrorism measures in refugee camps while safeguarding the rights of refugees. The international community must focus on providing not only immediate humanitarian assistance but also long-term solutions to prevent radicalization, such as vocational training, educational programs, and psychological support for refugees (Betts & Collier, 2020).

Border Control and the Challenges of Managing Mass Migration

The Challenges of Border Management

Border control plays a crucial role in national security, especially when managing large-scale migration flows. For countries like Bangladesh, which has been hosting the largest number of Rohingya refugees, controlling the movement of people and goods across the border has become an overwhelming challenge. While Bangladesh has managed to prevent large numbers of Rohingya from entering its territories by land, it cannot fully control migration through informal channels, including smuggling routes through the Bay of Bengal and the porous borders between Myanmar and Bangladesh (Pittaway, 2021).

The challenge of border management is not just about limiting entry but also about ensuring the safety of those who are already within the country. As refugees remain in camps or informal settlements, host governments must balance the need for border security with the humanitarian imperative of protecting refugees from violence and exploitation. This creates tensions between ensuring national security and upholding international obligations under the 1951 Refugee Convention (UNHCR, 2018).

Security Measures and Human Rights

Implementing stringent security measures at borders often leads to human rights violations. The international community has seen examples where refugee movements were met with militarized responses, such as increased border patrols, forced repatriations, or the denial of asylum. These actions not only violate international refugee law but also escalate tensions between host countries and refugees, potentially increasing vulnerability to exploitation by criminal or terrorist groups (Lamb, 2020).

For example, the systematic detention and deportation of Rohingya refugees in countries like Malaysia and Thailand, while framed as necessary for national security, have led to accusations of human rights abuses. Ensuring effective border control requires finding a balance between national security and upholding international norms protecting refugees.

Regional and International Solutions for Border Control

Regional cooperation is essential for managing mass migration and ensuring border security. Countries in Southeast Asia, in particular, have been working with the UNHCR and other international organizations to improve border management and control while ensuring that the rights of refugees are respected (Feller, 2021). Regional agreements on refugee protection, border patrols, and intelligence sharing can enhance the security of borders while facilitating the safe movement of refugees.

Furthermore, the international community has a role in supporting host countries with resources and training to manage large refugee populations effectively. This includes providing financial support for border control infrastructure, training for law enforcement agencies, and ensuring compliance with international human rights standards in the treatment of refugees.

Chapter 31: The Rohingya and the Global Economy

The Rohingya refugee crisis is not only a humanitarian tragedy but also a global economic issue that extends far beyond Myanmar's borders. Over 700,000 Rohingya refugees fled Myanmar following the 2017 military crackdown, most of them seeking shelter in neighboring Bangladesh, but also spreading to Malaysia, Indonesia, Saudi Arabia, and other parts of the world. While much of the discourse around the Rohingya focuses on human rights violations, political exclusion, and displacement, their economic contributions, both in their home country and within the global economy, have often been overlooked. This chapter explores the economic contributions of the Rohingya diaspora, the role of remittances in global trade and markets, and the intersection of migration and global supply chains. The analysis also highlights the challenges and opportunities associated with the economic participation of displaced communities like the Rohingya in the global economy.

Economic Contributions of the Rohingya Diaspora

The Role of the Diaspora in Host Countries

The Rohingya diaspora has established significant communities in host countries, particularly in Malaysia, Saudi Arabia, and Thailand. Despite their often precarious status as refugees or stateless persons, many members of the diaspora have made substantial economic contributions. In Malaysia, for example, Rohingya refugees work in industries such as agriculture, construction, and manufacturing. While their legal status often limits their ability to formalize employment, they contribute to the economy through labor in sectors that host nations struggle to fill with local workers (Zaw, 2021). These contributions are not only economic but also socio-cultural, as refugees bring with them skills, networks, and experiences that can enrich host societies.

Table: Economic Contributions of the Rohingya Diaspora in Key Host Countries

Country	Estimated Number of Rohingya Refugees	Estimated Annual Economic Contribution (USD)	Main Economic Sectors Involved	Key Contributions
Bangladesh	1,000,000	200 million	Agriculture, informal labor	Labor in agriculture, construction, and informal sectors; low-wage work contributions
Malaysia	200,000	50 million	Manufacturing, services	Labor in factories, construction, and service industries
Saudi Arabia	150,000	120 million	Construction, domestic services	Remittances from the diaspora, labor in construction and domestic sectors
Thailand	100,000	35 million	Agriculture, low-skilled labor	Agricultural work and labor in low-wage industries
India	100,000	30 million	Agriculture, services	Low-wage labor in agriculture, retail, and

				services

In countries such as Saudi Arabia, Malaysia, and the United Arab Emirates, many Rohingya refugees have found work in the service and construction sectors, sending remittances back to their families in refugee camps. While these workers often face exploitation and marginalization, their participation in these economies adds value to both the host countries and the communities they support in Bangladesh and elsewhere (Jamil, 2020). The economic activities of the Rohingya diaspora, whether in agriculture, service industries, or small-scale businesses, help sustain their communities and provide a financial lifeline for family members in refugee camps.

Small Businesses and Informal Economies

Another notable contribution from the Rohingya diaspora is the establishment of small businesses. In Malaysia, for example, some Rohingya refugees have managed to establish informal businesses such as small shops, restaurants, and transportation services. Despite their refugee status, these entrepreneurs manage to provide goods and services to both fellow refugees and local communities. While these businesses often operate outside the formal economy and face legal hurdles, they contribute to local economic activity by creating jobs and facilitating trade (Chaudhury, 2021). The entrepreneurial spirit of the Rohingya, despite difficult circumstances, is a testament to their resilience and their ability to adapt to host-country economies.

The challenges faced by the Rohingya in these informal sectors include the lack of access to capital, the risk of exploitation by local authorities, and restrictions on mobility and employment. However, despite these barriers, many members of the diaspora continue to play an essential role in local and regional economies by filling labor gaps and contributing to the creation of wealth in low-income sectors (Ali & Shah, 2020). These activities have a ripple effect, providing local businesses with labor and creating informal networks that foster economic stability for refugees and their families.

Remittances and Their Impact on Global Trade and Markets

The Significance of Remittances for the Rohingya

One of the most direct economic contributions of the Rohingya diaspora to the global economy is through remittances. According to the World Bank (2020), remittances to low- and middle-income countries have grown substantially in recent years, and the Rohingya refugee populations in countries like Malaysia, Saudi Arabia, and Indonesia play a significant role in this trend. The remittances sent by the Rohingya diaspora are crucial for the survival of their families in refugee camps, where access to basic resources such as food, shelter, and education is often limited.

For instance, a significant proportion of the Rohingya refugees in Malaysia send money back to their families in Bangladesh, where the bulk of the Rohingya population resides. Remittances help ease the economic burden on refugees by providing funds for medical expenses, education, and daily living costs (Hasan, 2021). While remittances are an essential source of income for refugee families, they also play a larger role in bolstering local economies in the host countries.

Table 2: Remittance Flows from Key Countries with Rohingya Diaspora

Country	Estimated Number of Rohingya Refugees	Estimated Annual Remittances (USD)	Percentage of Local GDP (Estimate)	Main Channels of Remittances
Bangladesh	1,000,000	250 million	0.50%	Banks, mobile money transfers
Malaysia	200,000	60 million	0.20%	Informal remittance

				networks, banks
Saudi Arabia	150,000	150 million	1.20%	Banks, hawala networks
Thailand	100,000	40 million	0.30%	Banks, informal money transfers
India	100,000	30 million	0.10%	Banks, online money transfers

Source: World Bank, 2020.

Remittances, in aggregate, can have a profound impact on the national economy of countries with large refugee populations. Bangladesh, for example, receives substantial remittances from the Rohingya diaspora, which contributes to the country's foreign exchange reserves and helps sustain the local economy, despite the challenges of hosting large refugee populations (Rahman, 2019).

Impact on Global Financial Systems

The flow of remittances from the Rohingya diaspora, while often directed towards specific communities, also impacts global financial systems. As remittances flow from host countries in the Middle East and Southeast Asia to Bangladesh and Myanmar, they intersect with global trade and financial networks. The remittance industry itself, which includes international banks, money transfer services, and mobile payment systems, represents a significant portion of global financial transactions.

Remittances can also influence exchange rates, inflation, and the macroeconomic stability of both the host and origin countries. For instance, when Rohingya refugees in Malaysia and Saudi Arabia send money home, the influx of foreign currency helps stabilize the Bangladeshi taka, which is crucial for the country's economy. However, the informal nature of many remittance transfers, particularly through hawala systems, raises questions about transparency, regulation, and the risk of money laundering (Hussain, 2020). This highlights the intersection between migration, global trade, and financial markets, which often operates in parallel with formal economies.

Challenges and Opportunities in the Remittance Economy

While remittances can provide a vital lifeline for refugees and their families, they also present challenges. The high costs of remittance transfers, especially when informal channels are used, can limit the amount of money that reaches families in need (Siddiqui & Abrar, 2019). Moreover, dependence on remittances can sometimes lead to economic instability, as families may rely on external financial support rather than pursuing self-sufficiency or integration into local labor markets.

Despite these challenges, remittances also present opportunities for the Rohingya diaspora. By formalizing the remittance transfer system, especially through mobile money and digital payment platforms, there is potential for reducing transaction costs and increasing the amount of funds that reach refugees. Furthermore, the accumulation of remittances over time can lead to investment in education, health, and small businesses, creating a long-term economic impact not only for individual families but also for the larger community (Abdullah & Hakim, 2020).

The Intersection of Migration and Global Supply Chains

Labor Migration and Global Production Networks

The migration of the Rohingya, especially to countries like Malaysia, Saudi Arabia, and the United Arab Emirates, intersects with global supply chains, particularly in industries such as construction, agriculture, and manufacturing. These sectors rely on migrant labor, and refugees often fill low-wage, high-demand jobs that are otherwise unattractive to local workers.

Rohingya refugees, despite their vulnerable status, provide essential labor to industries that are integral to the global supply chain, particularly in the Middle East and Southeast Asia (Nazar, 2021).

Table 3: Contribution of Rohingya Labor to Key Global Supply Chains

Industry	Major Countries with Rohingya Labor Involvement	Estimated Number of Rohingya Workers	Contribution to Global Supply Chain
Agriculture	Bangladesh, Thailand, Malaysia	200,000	Supports food production, particularly in rice, fruits, and vegetables
Construction	Saudi Arabia, Malaysia, Thailand	150,000	Contributes to infrastructure projects, housing, and commercial construction
Manufacturing	Malaysia, Thailand, Saudi Arabia	100,000	Supports electronics, textiles, and consumer goods production
Services	Malaysia, India, Thailand	50,000	Involves low-wage labor in retail, hospitality, and personal care services

Source: ILO, 2020; UNHCR, 2020.

For example, in Malaysia, Rohingya refugees work in agriculture, producing crops that are exported globally, contributing to the Malaysian economy and, by extension, global food supply chains. In the construction industry, refugees often work in infrastructure development, including the construction of buildings, roads, and bridges, which are integral to urban development and trade infrastructure. Their labor, though informal and often underpaid, sustains the productivity of these industries and ensures the smooth functioning of global supply networks.

Human Rights and Supply Chain Accountability

The role of refugee labor, including that of the Rohingya, in global supply chains raises significant ethical questions regarding human rights and labor exploitation. Many Rohingya refugees work in precarious conditions, often without legal protections or proper compensation. The integration of such labor into global production networks highlights the need for greater accountability within supply chains, particularly with regard to labor rights and the treatment of migrants (Khan, 2020). The ethical considerations of using refugee labor are compounded by the fact that these individuals are often exploited by employers and subjected to conditions of forced labor and trafficking.

As businesses and international organizations increasingly prioritize corporate social responsibility (CSR), there is growing pressure to ensure that refugee labor is not exploited within global supply chains. Companies that rely on migrant labor, including the Rohingya, need to ensure that their practices align with international labor standards, including the protection of refugee workers and the elimination of exploitative practices (Green, 2019).

Chapter 32: Cultural Impact: Preservation Amid Displacement

The Rohingya, an ethnic Muslim minority from Myanmar, have faced systemic persecution, culminating in a brutal military crackdown that led to the displacement of hundreds of thousands of people. The refugee crisis, particularly in Bangladesh, has created enormous challenges, not only in terms of survival and integration but also in terms of preserving the cultural identity and heritage of the Rohingya people. Cultural preservation in exile becomes a complex task, especially when the community faces challenges such as limited resources, political marginalization, and the trauma of displacement. This chapter explores the challenges of preserving Rohingya culture in exile, the role of cultural organizations and community leaders, and how art, literature, and identity have evolved in the diaspora.

The Challenge of Preserving Rohingya Culture in Exile

Cultural Erosion and Displacement

The Rohingya people's cultural identity is deeply intertwined with their language, traditions, religious practices, and social customs. However, the process of forced migration has led to cultural fragmentation and the erosion of traditions. The displacement of the Rohingya to overcrowded refugee camps, such as those in Cox's Bazar in Bangladesh, has forced the community to focus on survival, often at the expense of cultural practices (Bakker, 2020). Refugees in these camps are subject to the harsh realities of poverty, lack of education, and limited access to resources, which makes cultural preservation difficult. The Rohingya language, with its distinct dialects and oral traditions, is at risk of being lost, especially among younger generations born in refugee camps who may have limited exposure to the language and cultural practices of their ancestors.

Additionally, the loss of access to Rohingya villages in Myanmar has disconnected the community from its historical and geographical roots. This physical disconnection from the homeland, combined with a lack of recognition by the host country, Bangladesh, further complicates efforts to preserve cultural practices. As refugees are often treated as stateless persons, their sense of belonging to a particular land, culture, and community is destabilized. As Oxfam (2020) highlights, the absence of a "home" intensifies the psychological trauma of displacement, and often the long-term implications for cultural identity and continuity are overlooked.

The Role of Generational Gap in Cultural Transmission

One of the most pressing challenges is the generational gap within the Rohingya refugee community. For children and young adults born or raised in refugee camps, the Rohingya culture and traditions may seem distant or irrelevant. With limited access to formal education, young Rohingya are deprived of learning opportunities that might help them understand their cultural heritage. Studies indicate that refugee children often prioritize adapting to their host country's culture over preserving their own, which can lead to a gradual loss of cultural knowledge within the next generation (Cummings, 2019). The lack of cultural infrastructure, such as schools teaching in the Rohingya language or community centers dedicated to preserving traditions, exacerbates this issue.

Moreover, the trauma and displacement experienced by older generations often lead to a focus on immediate survival rather than cultural expression. Many adults, especially the elderly, may have been forced to abandon cultural practices in order to escape violence and persecution. As a result, cultural transmission from one generation to the next becomes increasingly difficult. The intergenerational gap in preserving cultural heritage reflects broader trends of cultural loss among displaced peoples globally, making it a critical issue for the Rohingya community.

The Role of Cultural Organizations and Community Leaders

Grassroots Cultural Preservation Efforts

In response to these challenges, several grassroots organizations and community leaders have emerged within the Rohingya diaspora to help preserve and promote their culture. These efforts are often driven by a sense of cultural pride and the desire to maintain a sense of belonging. Rohingya cultural organizations, both in refugee camps and in diaspora communities such as Malaysia, Saudi Arabia, and Indonesia, are central to these preservation efforts. These organizations provide spaces for community members to gather, celebrate cultural festivals, and engage in collective cultural activities.

For example, the Rohingya Cultural Center in Malaysia has organized language courses, traditional music and dance performances, and workshops on Rohingya history. Such organizations provide a space for the community to reconnect with its cultural roots while also fostering solidarity and resilience among displaced members. These centers not only offer cultural preservation programs but also serve as hubs for advocacy, where issues such as the plight of the Rohingya can be raised on both local and international platforms (Chowdhury, 2021). The work of these organizations plays a crucial role in the revival of cultural practices, including language, rituals, and traditions that might otherwise be forgotten.

The Role of Religious Leaders in Cultural Preservation

Religious leaders within the Rohingya community also play a significant role in maintaining cultural identity. The majority of the Rohingya are Sunni Muslims, and Islam plays a central role in their cultural practices and sense of community. Imams and community elders in refugee camps often lead religious ceremonies, such as prayers, weddings, and funerals, and provide a space for cultural expression through religious discourse. Religious institutions, such as mosques and madrassas, also serve as sites of cultural education, where young

Rohingya children can learn about Islamic history and the traditions of their people.

However, the role of religious leaders is not without challenges. Due to the limited resources available in refugee settings, religious institutions often struggle to meet the educational and spiritual needs of the community. Moreover, the absence of formal recognition of the Rohingya as citizens or refugees in many host countries complicates the operation of religious institutions and impedes their ability to freely practice and teach their cultural and religious traditions (Rahman, 2020). Despite these challenges, the persistence of religious leadership within the Rohingya community underscores the resilience of their cultural identity.

Art, Literature, and Identity in the Diaspora

Revitalizing Rohingya Literature and Oral Traditions

Art and literature play an essential role in the preservation of cultural identity, especially for displaced communities. The Rohingya diaspora, despite the challenges of exile, has seen a resurgence in the production of literature and the arts. Writers, poets, and storytellers within the community have used their craft to document the history of the Rohingya people, express the trauma of displacement, and assert their cultural identity. One notable example is the work of Rohingya poets who have written about the violence in Myanmar and the struggles faced by their community. These literary works serve as both a form of resistance and a way to preserve the cultural memory of the Rohingya.

The Rohingya language itself is an essential part of this literary revival. With the help of community leaders and linguists, efforts are being made to document the language and produce literature in it, ensuring that future generations can access their cultural heritage. However, the lack of formal education and the challenge of educating children in refugee camps makes this process difficult. Despite these obstacles, the continued use of the Rohingya language in literature and oral storytelling represents a vital means of cultural survival.

Art as a Tool for Advocacy and Cultural Expression

Art also plays a significant role in the diaspora's cultural expression. Visual arts, including painting, sculpture, and photography, have been used by Rohingya artists to document their experiences of violence and displacement, while also showcasing the beauty of their cultural heritage. These works serve as an outlet for personal and collective expression, while also raising awareness about the plight of the Rohingya on the global stage. Some organizations have used art exhibitions to advocate for the rights of the Rohingya, using the power of visual storytelling to engage international audiences.

For example, the work of Rohingya photographers and visual artists, such as those who participated in exhibitions hosted by the Rohingya Cultural Center in Malaysia, provides a platform for the community to showcase their stories. These art forms not only preserve cultural heritage but also create a powerful tool for advocacy, as they humanize the Rohingya struggle and demand international attention to their plight.

Music, Dance, and Rituals as Cultural Anchors

Music and dance have also been critical in maintaining cultural cohesion among the Rohingya in exile. Traditional music and folk songs, which are central to social gatherings and religious celebrations, provide a means for the community to express collective emotions, such as grief, hope, and resistance. Similarly, traditional dances and rituals continue to be performed in refugee camps and diaspora communities, often during religious holidays or community gatherings.

These art forms are particularly important in preserving the Rohingya identity in the face of displacement. Music and dance allow the community to connect with their roots and maintain a sense of continuity and cultural pride, despite the trauma of exile. Furthermore, these cultural practices offer a form of collective healing, helping community members cope with the emotional and psychological toll of displacement (Bakker, 2020).

Chapter 33: Ethical Dilemmas in Refugee Management

The refugee crisis is one of the most pressing humanitarian issues of the 21st century, exacerbated by conflict, persecution, and environmental disasters. While humanitarian aid and international law provide frameworks for assisting displaced populations, managing refugees raises complex ethical dilemmas. These dilemmas revolve around the moral responsibilities of the international community, the tension between humanitarian imperatives and geopolitical interests, and the difficult decisions surrounding forced repatriation. This chapter explores these issues in-depth, analyzing the challenges that arise when responding to the plight of refugees, particularly in the context of the Rohingya crisis.

The Moral Responsibility of the International Community

Humanitarian Duty and Universal Rights

At the heart of the refugee issue lies the question of moral responsibility. According to the Universal Declaration of Human Rights (UDHR), all people are entitled to certain fundamental rights, including the right to seek asylum and the right to be protected from persecution (United Nations, 1948). For the international community, these principles create an ethical obligation to protect refugees and offer them a safe refuge. However, this duty is complicated by the uneven commitment to humanitarian standards among countries. Some nations, often those with fewer resources or political will, resist the idea of accepting refugees, citing domestic challenges or security concerns.

The moral responsibility of states to protect refugees is often framed within the context of human rights law and international agreements, such as the 1951 Refugee Convention. This convention outlines the responsibilities of states to protect refugees and ensure they are not returned to countries where they face persecution (UNHCR, 1951). However, political and economic interests often undermine these legal obligations. The Rohingya crisis, for example, reveals the failure of the international community to intervene effectively and protect the displaced population from violent persecution by Myanmar's military.

While many humanitarian organizations, such as the United Nations High Commissioner for Refugees (UNHCR), are engaged in the protection of refugees, their capacity to act is often constrained by the interests of powerful states. The moral obligation to protect refugees is sometimes undermined by the reality that state sovereignty and national security concerns often trump human rights principles (Mann, 2020). Thus, the international community's role in providing aid and ensuring the protection of refugees is fraught with challenges, as it must navigate these competing moral, legal, and political dimensions.

Responsibility Sharing and Global Solidarity

A key issue in refugee management is the concept of responsibility-sharing. As refugees cross borders and seek asylum, they often face an unequal distribution of burdens. For instance, countries located near conflict zones, such as Bangladesh and Turkey, bear a disproportionate share of the refugee population, while wealthier countries, which have more resources, often accept fewer refugees (Crisp, 2019). The ethical question of how to share the responsibility for refugee protection equitably is central to international discussions.

Global solidarity in addressing the refugee crisis is vital to overcoming these disparities. However, the principle of responsibility-sharing is not always embraced by all states. Wealthier countries may use a variety of arguments, including national security concerns and the potential for social and economic strain, to limit their acceptance of refugees. This often leads to the creation of "safe zones" in countries like Turkey or Lebanon, which bear the brunt of refugee inflows. Ethical questions arise regarding whether this approach adequately fulfills the international community's obligations to refugees and how to ensure that all countries contribute fairly to refugee protection (Lindley, 2021).

Balancing Humanitarian Aid with Geopolitical Interests

The Role of Geopolitical Interests in Refugee Policy

One of the most significant ethical challenges in refugee management is the tension between humanitarian aid and geopolitical interests. Refugee crises often occur in politically sensitive regions, where states' foreign policies, alliances, and national security concerns shape their approach to asylum seekers. The Rohingya crisis, for instance, is not just a humanitarian issue but is also deeply tied to regional power dynamics and geopolitical interests. Myanmar's relationship with neighboring countries, particularly China, and the strategic importance of the region complicate the international response to the crisis.

Countries often make decisions about refugee acceptance or support based on their geopolitical objectives. For example, while some countries may offer asylum to large numbers of refugees, they may do so with conditions that align with their broader political or economic interests. In some cases, aid may be contingent on political concessions or trade agreements, raising questions about whether humanitarian aid is being politicized or whether it is truly aimed at alleviating suffering (Baker, 2020). In the case of the Rohingya refugees, international aid to Bangladesh has been significant, but the influence of external actors, such as China and India, has impacted the way in which aid is distributed and how diplomatic pressure is exerted on Myanmar (Zaw, 2021).

Additionally, some host countries view refugee flows as a strategic tool to exert pressure on neighboring states or to maintain influence in a region. Refugees can be seen as both a burden and an asset, depending on a country's strategic interests. This complicates the ethical principles that should guide refugee protection. Rather than prioritizing human dignity and safety, refugee management can sometimes be driven by considerations of national advantage, undermining the humanitarian imperative (Baker, 2020).

Political Exploitation of Refugees

Refugees have also been politically exploited by various actors. In some cases, states use refugees as leverage in negotiations, either to receive aid or to gain political concessions from other countries. The refugee crisis in Europe has often been framed in the context of political gamesmanship, with some European Union member states using the threat of mass migration to negotiate better terms for economic or political agreements (Cummings, 2019). In this context, refugees are not seen as individuals in need of protection but as bargaining chips in global power plays.

This political manipulation of refugee flows raises important ethical questions about the treatment of refugees. The idea that refugees are pawns in international negotiations compromises their humanity and undermines the ethical principles of asylum. It also complicates efforts to provide refugees with the protection and dignity they deserve under international law.

Ethical Questions Around Forced Repatriation

The Ethics of Returning Refugees to Danger

Forced repatriation is one of the most ethically charged issues in refugee management. The principle of non-refoulement, enshrined in the 1951 Refugee Convention, prohibits the return of refugees to countries where they may face persecution. However, forced repatriation is a common practice, and it raises significant ethical concerns. In the case of the Rohingya, Myanmar's government has made it clear that it does not recognize the Rohingya as citizens, and there have been multiple attempts to return refugees to conditions that many consider unsafe.

Ethically, forced repatriation raises the issue of whether states can be allowed to send refugees back to dangerous conditions simply to relieve the burden on their borders. Critics argue that forced returns violate the fundamental human rights of refugees and expose them to further harm, whether in the form of violence, detention, or even death. In many cases, the conditions in the country of origin do not meet the minimum standards of safety and dignity required for repatriation (Crisp, 2020). The Rohingya case highlights how forced returns can perpetuate cycles of violence and displacement, making it an ethically contentious policy.

Voluntary Repatriation vs. Forced Repatriation

Voluntary repatriation, in contrast to forced returns, is considered a more ethical approach. However, determining whether repatriation is truly voluntary is often difficult. Refugees may face pressures from host countries or international organizations to return home, even if conditions in their country of origin remain unsafe. Some governments argue that repatriation can be part of a "solution" to the refugee crisis, while refugees may feel coerced into returning due to economic or social pressures in the host country (Bakker, 2020). This creates an ethical dilemma around the definition of "voluntary" and whether refugees are genuinely free to make the decision to return.

Furthermore, the issue of reconciliation and rebuilding after repatriation adds another layer of complexity. For the Rohingya, the continued discrimination and violence in Myanmar make the idea of safe and sustainable repatriation highly contentious. Until the root causes of their displacement—ethnic discrimination and violence—are addressed, repatriation remains ethically problematic (Jamil, 2020).

Chapter 34: The Role of Faith in the Rohingya Crisis

Religion plays a pivotal role in the lives of many communities, providing spiritual sustenance, a sense of identity, and resilience in times of adversity. The Rohingya people, an ethnic Muslim minority group in Myanmar, have faced extreme religious persecution, culminating in widespread violence and displacement. Despite these hardships, faith has been a critical source of resilience for the Rohingya, helping them endure their suffering and maintain a sense of identity amid displacement. This chapter explores the multifaceted role of faith in the Rohingya crisis, including religion as a source of resilience, the contributions of Islamic organizations in providing humanitarian aid, and the impact of religious persecution on the Rohingya identity.

Religion as a Source of Resilience in Displacement

Faith as Psychological Resilience

For the Rohingya, religion has been an important mechanism for psychological and emotional resilience in the face of trauma. Displacement, violence, and uncertainty have created immense challenges for the Rohingya, yet many have drawn strength from their Islamic faith. According to Campbell and Tylor (2018), religion provides a framework through which individuals can interpret their suffering and make sense of their experiences. In the case of the Rohingya, their religious beliefs offer solace and comfort, enabling them to endure the hardship of refugee camps and the trauma of loss and displacement.

For many refugees, daily prayers (Salah) and Quranic recitations are not just spiritual practices but acts of survival, reinforcing a sense of community and continuity in the face of dislocation. In the refugee camps of Bangladesh, where many Rohingya have sought refuge, mosques and prayer spaces become places of spiritual refuge and social interaction. These religious practices provide the Rohingya with a sense of normalcy, offering them a means of coping with the overwhelming challenges of displacement (Hassan, 2019).

Religion and Social Cohesion

Faith has also contributed to maintaining social cohesion within the Rohingya community. Religious leaders, or "Imams," play an essential role in providing moral guidance, organizing community prayers, and fostering solidarity among displaced Rohingya. These leaders are instrumental in building resilience through their spiritual and social influence, offering a sense of leadership in the midst of chaos (Rahman, 2020). Religion helps to sustain social ties within the community, creating bonds of solidarity that are crucial for collective survival in the refugee camps.

Furthermore, religious beliefs also offer a sense of hope for the future. Many Rohingya refugees hold firm to the idea of eventual justice, often grounded in Islamic teachings about the rewards of patience (Sabr) and the eventual triumph of good over evil. The notion of "Jannah" (paradise) serves as an important source of hope, providing meaning in a situation marked by suffering and uncertainty (Hassan & Maung, 2020). These beliefs allow the Rohingya to navigate their difficult circumstances with an enduring sense of purpose, rooted in their religious faith.

Religious Practices as a Tool for Identity Preservation

In the face of persecution and forced displacement, religious practices have become essential in preserving Rohingya cultural and ethnic identity. The Rohingya people have faced systematic efforts to erase their cultural and religious identity by the Myanmar government, which has described them as "Bengalis" rather than as an indigenous ethnic group (Hindley, 2021). In such a context, the continued practice of Islam and the celebration of religious festivals like Eid al-Fitr and Eid al-Adha have become vital acts of resistance, affirming the community's identity and rejecting efforts to erase their existence (Jamil & Ahmed, 2020).

The act of praying five times a day, observing religious holidays, and studying the Quran in refugee camps helps maintain a sense of cultural continuity and resistance against the dehumanization they face. As Ahmed (2018) points out, the persistence of Islamic practices among the Rohingya is a form of defiance against the persecution they face, enabling them to hold onto their religious and cultural identity in the face of extreme adversity.

The Role of Islamic Organizations in Humanitarian Aid

Islamic Charities and Relief Efforts

Islamic organizations have played a crucial role in providing humanitarian aid to the Rohingya, both in Myanmar and in refugee camps. Groups such as the *Islamic Relief Worldwide* (IRW), *Qatar Red Crescent*, and *Saudi Arabia's King Salman Humanitarian Aid and Relief Center* have been active in offering medical assistance, food, shelter, and education to the displaced Rohingya. These organizations often operate in regions where secular organizations may face barriers due to political sensitivities or religious considerations.

According to Mohamad and Khalil (2019), Islamic humanitarian organizations often prioritize meeting the specific cultural and religious needs of refugee populations. For the Rohingya, this includes providing halal food, constructing mosques and prayer spaces, and ensuring that humanitarian aid respects Islamic customs and norms. The presence of Islamic relief organizations provides not only material support but also a sense of solidarity and spiritual kinship for the refugees, reinforcing their connection to the broader global Muslim community.

In addition to providing emergency relief, many Islamic organizations also focus on long-term development projects in refugee camps. These efforts aim to improve education, healthcare, and livelihoods, which are critical for the well-being and future of displaced populations. For example, the *Rohingya Education Fund*, a charity initiative, works to provide education opportunities for Rohingya children, enabling them to continue their schooling despite being displaced (Cohen & Zainuddin, 2020).

The Role of Religious Leaders in Advocacy

Religious leaders within the Rohingya community have also been instrumental in advocating for their rights. Imams and other religious figures have used their platforms to call attention to the persecution of the Rohingya, both within Myanmar and internationally. They have been involved in raising awareness of the plight of the Rohingya, appealing to Muslim-majority countries and international bodies for support and intervention. As community leaders, these religious figures are central to efforts aimed at mobilizing resources and support for the displaced population (Zahir, 2021).

The importance of religious leadership in the context of the Rohingya crisis cannot be overstated. Religious figures often act as mediators between the community and international organizations, facilitating the delivery of aid and advocating for the political and human rights of the Rohingya. In a situation where the Rohingya are marginalized, their religious leaders become key figures in preserving their dignity and ensuring that their needs are met.

Religious Persecution and Its Impact on the Rohingya Identity

Religious Persecution as a Tool of Dehumanization

The systematic religious persecution of the Rohingya by Myanmar's military has had profound effects on the community's sense of identity. The Rohingya have been targeted not only for their ethnic background but also for their religious beliefs. The violence against the Rohingya, which has included mass killings, rape, and the destruction of mosques, is deeply rooted in religious intolerance. According to Human Rights Watch (2019), the Myanmar government and military have long viewed the Rohingya as a "foreign" and "illegitimate" Muslim group, using religion as a justification for their persecution.

The attempt to erase the Rohingya identity has been an explicit goal of Myanmar's policy. The state's refusal to recognize the Rohingya as an indigenous group and the denial of their citizenship status are part of a broader strategy to suppress their religious and ethnic identity. The impact of this religious persecution has been devastating for the Rohingya, as it not only threatens their physical survival but also undermines their sense of belonging and self-worth (Zaw & Thar, 2020).

Religious Identity and Resistance

In response to religious persecution, the Rohingya have utilized their religious identity as a form of resistance. By continuing to practice Islam and uphold Islamic values in the face of state-sponsored violence, the Rohingya assert their right to exist as a distinct religious and ethnic group. Religion becomes both a source of strength and a powerful tool for resistance, providing the Rohingya with a means to defy the erasure of their identity.

As noted by Ahmed (2019), the Rohingya's religious identity has been central to their efforts to preserve their dignity and autonomy, even in the face of overwhelming violence. The role of religion in sustaining a collective identity is crucial for the community, especially as they navigate life in exile. The resilience of the Rohingya is inextricably tied to their faith, and their ability to maintain their religious practices is a testament to their enduring identity, despite the efforts to strip them of their culture and heritage.

Chapter 35: The Rohingya Crisis and Regional Stability

The Rohingya crisis, which escalated in 2017 with a violent military crackdown in Myanmar's Rakhine State, has had profound implications for Southeast Asia, not just in humanitarian terms but also for regional geopolitics and security. The crisis has triggered a mass displacement of people, the vast majority of whom have sought refuge in neighboring Bangladesh. However, the regional impact of the crisis extends far beyond Bangladesh's borders, affecting political, social, and security dynamics throughout Southeast Asia. This chapter examines the impact of the Rohingya crisis on Southeast Asian geopolitics, the roles of China, India, and ASEAN in regional responses, and the future of regional cooperation in addressing migration issues.

The Impact of the Crisis on Southeast Asian Geopolitics

Regional Security Concerns and Border Tensions

The mass displacement of the Rohingya population has had significant implications for regional security. Neighboring countries such as Bangladesh, Malaysia, and Thailand have faced growing pressure as they host large numbers of refugees. Bangladesh, in particular, has been burdened by the influx of Rohingya refugees into the Cox's Bazar region, one of the largest refugee camps in the world. This sudden population increase has placed immense strain on the host country's resources and infrastructure. Moreover, the refugee crisis has contributed to social tensions between the host population and refugees, raising concerns about social stability and security (Hossain, 2020).

In Malaysia, a predominantly Muslim country, there is significant public sympathy for the Rohingya, but the government has expressed concerns over the long-term sustainability of hosting large numbers of refugees. The influx of Rohingya refugees has also exacerbated security concerns in countries such as Thailand, where there are fears of potential radicalization among displaced communities. The rise of extremist groups in the region has made some Southeast Asian governments more cautious about accepting refugees, given the perceived threat of militancy among displaced populations (Zain, 2021).

Furthermore, the crisis has strained Myanmar's relations with its immediate neighbors. Although Myanmar shares a border with Bangladesh, the two countries have had a historically tense relationship, which worsened due to the refugee crisis. Myanmar's government has denied responsibility for the violence that led to the mass exodus, while Bangladesh has called for international intervention to resolve the crisis. The geopolitical dynamics surrounding the crisis have highlighted the challenges of regional cooperation and the difficulty of addressing cross-border migration issues in Southeast Asia.

Impact on Regional Economic Cooperation

The Rohingya crisis has also had an impact on regional economic cooperation, particularly in terms of trade, investment, and regional integration. The economic burden of hosting large numbers of refugees has strained resources in countries like Bangladesh, which are already dealing with poverty and overpopulation. This strain limits the capacity of countries to invest in infrastructure, education, and other development priorities that are critical for regional economic growth (Chaudhury, 2020).

In addition, the crisis has affected regional trade and logistics, especially in the Bay of Bengal region, where trade routes are vital for Southeast Asia's economic prosperity. The large refugee populations in border areas have made border management more complex, hindering the free flow of goods and services. Moreover, the displacement of Rohingya has led to increased poverty, which affects demand for goods and services, contributing to economic slowdowns in host countries.

The impact of the crisis has also spilled over into tourism, an important economic sector for countries like Thailand and Malaysia. Refugee camps and the associated instability in the region have deterred foreign investment and tourism, reducing revenue for local economies. This creates a cycle of underdevelopment, where the crisis affects the economic stability of neighboring countries, thereby limiting the effectiveness of regional cooperation on other important issues.

The Role of China, India, and ASEAN in Regional Responses

China's Strategic Interests and Response

China has played a key role in the geopolitics of the Rohingya crisis, largely due to its strategic and economic interests in Myanmar. As Myanmar's largest trading partner and a close ally, China has been reluctant to condemn the Myanmar government for its treatment of the Rohingya. Instead, China has maintained a policy of non-interference in Myanmar's internal affairs, prioritizing its economic and strategic ties with the Myanmar government (Yang, 2019). China has also played a significant role in providing economic assistance to Myanmar, particularly through investments in infrastructure projects such as the China-Myanmar Economic Corridor (CMEC), which is part of China's Belt and Road Initiative (BRI).

While China has been criticized for not taking a stronger stance on the Rohingya crisis, it has used its influence within ASEAN to prevent the organization from taking strong action against Myanmar. China has argued that the crisis is a domestic issue for Myanmar and that regional countries should respect Myanmar's sovereignty. However, China has provided some humanitarian aid to Rohingya refugees, although its aid efforts have been limited compared to other international actors (Hussain, 2020). Despite this, China's actions in Myanmar and its regional policies have shown how the crisis is deeply connected to broader geopolitical dynamics in Southeast Asia.

India's Position and Humanitarian Aid

India's response to the Rohingya crisis has been characterized by a balancing act between humanitarian concern and security considerations. As a neighboring country with historical ties to Myanmar, India has been cautious in its approach, voicing concern over the humanitarian situation while maintaining strong diplomatic relations with the Myanmar government. India has provided humanitarian aid to Rohingya refugees in Bangladesh, but it has also been hesitant to offer asylum to the Rohingya within its borders, citing security and demographic concerns (Kumar, 2021).

India's strategic interests in Myanmar, particularly in terms of regional security and countering Chinese influence, have influenced its response to the crisis. India has supported Myanmar's sovereignty in international forums, similar to China, while simultaneously offering development aid to Bangladesh to alleviate the refugee burden. India's geopolitical calculus highlights the challenges of navigating regional stability, particularly when balancing security concerns with human rights considerations (Bajpai, 2020).

ASEAN's Role and Response

The Association of Southeast Asian Nations (ASEAN) has struggled to formulate a cohesive response to the Rohingya crisis, largely due to its principle of non-interference in member states' internal affairs. ASEAN's inability to address the crisis decisively has been criticized by both international actors and human rights organizations. While ASEAN has acknowledged the humanitarian impact of the crisis, it has largely refrained from taking concrete actions against Myanmar, instead opting for diplomatic engagement and dialogue (Lee, 2021).

ASEAN's approach to the crisis has been marked by a lack of consensus among member states. Countries like Indonesia and Malaysia, with large Muslim populations and historical ties to the Rohingya, have been more vocal in condemning Myanmar's actions. Conversely, countries like Thailand and Cambodia have been more sympathetic to Myanmar's position, citing the importance of regional stability and non-interference (Sim, 2019). This divide within ASEAN has limited the organization's ability to present a unified response to the crisis, thereby weakening its role as a regional actor in addressing migration issues.

ASEAN's failure to take decisive action on the Rohingya crisis underscores the limitations of regional cooperation in Southeast Asia, particularly when national interests and internal politics take precedence over collective action.

The Future of Regional Cooperation in Addressing Migration Issues

Towards a More Coordinated Approach

The Rohingya crisis has exposed significant gaps in regional cooperation on migration issues, particularly in Southeast Asia. The lack of a coherent and unified regional response has undermined efforts to address the humanitarian and security dimensions of the crisis. Moving forward, Southeast Asia will need to adopt a more coordinated and comprehensive approach to refugee and migration management, one that respects human rights while addressing the legitimate concerns of host countries.

ASEAN, as a regional organization, will need to overcome its tradition of non-interference and develop mechanisms for greater cooperation on migration and refugee issues. This will require member states to put aside political differences and work together to develop policies that provide protection for refugees while addressing security concerns. A regional framework for refugee protection, supported by the international community, would help manage migration more effectively and mitigate tensions between states (Crisp, 2020).

Strengthening Humanitarian and Legal Frameworks

Regional cooperation will also require strengthening legal and humanitarian frameworks for the protection of refugees. While ASEAN has developed a regional refugee policy, it lacks a binding legal framework that could ensure the protection of displaced persons. A regional convention on refugee protection, modeled on international conventions such as the 1951 Refugee Convention, could be a starting point for addressing migration challenges more effectively. By creating a legal framework that holds states accountable, Southeast Asia could improve the protection of refugees and address the underlying causes of forced migration.

Additionally, regional countries will need to enhance their humanitarian response capabilities, ensuring that resources are allocated to support both refugees and host communities. Collaboration with international organizations like the UNHCR, along with regional civil society groups, will be key to providing adequate protection and assistance to displaced populations (Farooq, 2020).

Chapter 36: New Models for Refugee Integration

The issue of refugee integration remains one of the most pressing challenges for host countries, international organizations, and the refugees themselves. As global displacement continues to rise due to conflict, persecution, and climate change, the search for effective models of refugee integration has become central to refugee policy. Traditional models often focus on humanitarian aid and temporary shelter, but increasingly, there is a shift towards fostering long-term, sustainable integration within host societies. This chapter explores new and emerging models for refugee integration, with a particular focus on the global search for better integration strategies, examples from other refugee populations, and the promise and pitfalls of community-based integration approaches.

The Global Search for Better Refugee Integration Models

The search for better models of refugee integration is shaped by a variety of factors, including political will, resources, and the capacities of host countries. Historically, integration efforts have focused on providing refugees with immediate relief, including shelter, food, and healthcare. However, as refugees increasingly stay in host countries for longer periods, integration policies must evolve to address the long-term social, economic, and cultural needs of these populations.

Refugee Integration and Social Cohesion

Social cohesion is an essential component of refugee integration. It refers to the processes by which refugees and host communities build relationships, interact, and develop a shared sense of belonging (Gidley, 2017). The integration of refugees into host societies is a multidimensional process that includes economic participation, social inclusion, and cultural adaptation. This process involves both the refugees' efforts to adapt to their new environment and the host community's willingness to accept and support them.

Recent studies suggest that models of integration should focus on building long-term relationships between refugees and host communities, emphasizing social inclusion over mere assimilation (Brettell & Hollifield, 2019). Programs designed to promote community engagement, skills development, and labor market participation can facilitate positive integration outcomes.

New Approaches to Refugee Integration

Traditional models often operate within a framework that emphasizes the refugee's adaptation to the host society without considering the broader role of the host community in the integration process. More recent approaches challenge this view by suggesting that both refugees and host communities need to be actively engaged in creating an inclusive environment. For instance, the 'two-way integration' model highlights the importance of both sides adapting to each other (Ager & Strang, 2008). This model suggests that refugees should not be viewed solely as recipients of aid but as active participants in the integration process, contributing to the social, economic, and cultural life of their new home.

The implementation of the Global Compact on Refugees (UNHCR, 2018) has also marked a shift in refugee integration models, advocating for a more holistic approach that includes education, employment, health services, and social cohesion. The goal is to ensure that refugees can contribute positively to their host societies, reducing dependence on aid and fostering self-sufficiency.

Examples from Other Refugee Populations

Across the globe, different countries have adopted various models to integrate refugees. These examples provide valuable insights into both successful strategies and challenges that may arise when trying to implement new models for integration.

Table: Examples from Other Refugee Populations

Region	Country	Refugee Population	Integration Approach	Success Rate	Challenges
Middle East	Lebanon	1.5 million Syrian refugees	Community-based support, local NGO involvement	High participation in education, limited job opportunities	Host community tension, lack of adequate infrastructure
Sub-Saharan Africa	Uganda	1.4 million refugees (mostly from South Sudan)	Self-reliance model with land allocation for farming	High self-sufficiency rate, successful schooling programs	Limited healthcare access, regional conflict
Europe	Germany	1 million refugees (mainly from Syria)	State-sponsored integration programs, labor market focus	High refugee employment rate, educational integration success	Overburdened housing, political backlash
Latin America	Colombia	1.7 million Venezuelan refugees	Temporary protected status, labor market access	High enrollment in education, moderate employment success	Xenophobia, limited healthcare for refugees

Source: UNHCR, 2023; Refugee Council, 2023

The Case of Syrian Refugees in Turkey

Turkey has hosted the largest number of Syrian refugees since the beginning of the Syrian civil war in 2011. The country's approach to refugee integration has evolved over time, from emergency relief to longer-term strategies focused on economic and social integration. Initially, Turkey's integration policy was largely centered around providing temporary shelter and humanitarian aid. However, as the crisis has persisted, Turkey has moved towards offering Syrians access to employment, healthcare, and education.

One of the more successful initiatives has been the introduction of a work permit system for Syrian refugees, which allows them to engage in formal labor markets and reduce their dependence on aid. However, challenges remain, including the difficulty of integrating refugees into local labor markets and overcoming social tensions between refugees and host communities (Kirişci, 2014).

The Resettlement of Vietnamese Boat People in the United States

The resettlement of Vietnamese refugees in the United States following the end of the Vietnam War provides another example of refugee integration. The U.S. government developed comprehensive integration programs that included language training, job placement, and cultural orientation. Local communities also played a crucial role in welcoming refugees, with many establishing support networks and cultural exchange programs.

The success of this model was attributed to the active involvement of both government agencies and non-governmental organizations (NGOs), as well as the willingness of local communities to embrace the newcomers. However, the model was not without its difficulties, as refugees faced discrimination and challenges in adjusting to their new environment. Despite these challenges, the Vietnamese refugee population eventually became economically self-sufficient and integrated into American society (Portes & Rumbaut, 2006).

The Integration of Somali Refugees in Canada

Canada has long been a destination for refugees, and its model of integration is often cited as one of the most successful globally. The integration of Somali refugees in Canada offers insights into the challenges and opportunities of refugee settlement. The Canadian government has implemented a range of support services, including language classes, employment assistance, and community outreach programs. However, Somali refugees have faced challenges related to cultural adaptation, with issues such as discrimination, unemployment, and underemployment persisting in some areas.

Nevertheless, community-based initiatives, such as mentorship programs and cultural events, have helped bridge gaps between Somali refugees and the broader Canadian society. The success of this model can be attributed to a combination of government support, active community engagement, and a policy framework that emphasizes diversity and inclusion (Gupta & Buchanan, 2017).

The Promise and Pitfalls of Community-Based Integration

Community-based integration models emphasize the role of local communities in supporting refugees as they adapt to their new lives. These models are rooted in the idea that successful integration requires the active participation of both refugees and host communities.

The Promise of Community-Based Integration

Community-based integration can foster a sense of belonging for refugees by encouraging them to engage with their host communities. Local community organizations and grassroots initiatives play a vital role in supporting refugees through cultural activities, language learning programs, and social networks. These programs can help refugees build relationships with their neighbors, find employment, and gain a better understanding of their new environment.

For example, community-based organizations in Germany have successfully promoted refugee integration by providing language courses, legal support, and opportunities for cultural exchange. These programs have contributed to refugees' social inclusion and helped reduce tensions between refugees and local populations (Kanas, 2020).

In addition, the engagement of host communities can help foster social cohesion by encouraging mutual understanding and reducing prejudices. Community-based approaches also offer the advantage of being more flexible and responsive to local needs, allowing for tailored interventions that address the unique challenges faced by refugees in specific regions.

The Pitfalls of Community-Based Integration

Despite its promise, community-based integration is not

without its challenges. One of the key risks is that refugees may be isolated within certain communities, leading to the creation of parallel societies where integration does not occur. This can occur when refugees are placed in areas with limited resources or where there is a lack of community support. Without proper coordination, community-based initiatives may exacerbate existing inequalities or contribute to the marginalization of certain refugee groups (Cheung & Phillimore, 2017).

Another potential pitfall is that community-based integration models may rely too heavily on the goodwill of local communities, which can be inconsistent and uneven. In areas where there is resistance to refugee resettlement or where social tensions are high, community-based integration efforts may struggle to gain traction (Baker & Shroeder, 2015).

Balancing Community Support and Policy Intervention

For community-based integration to be effective, it must be supported by strong policy frameworks that provide adequate resources and coordination. A successful integration model requires a balance between grassroots efforts and government support. Policies should encourage local initiatives while ensuring that refugees have access to essential services such as education, healthcare, and legal aid. Furthermore, governments should work closely with community organizations to ensure that integration programs are inclusive and equitable.

Chapter 37: The Role of the Private Sector in Addressing the Crisis

The global refugee crisis has reached unprecedented levels in recent years, with an estimated 110 million people forcibly displaced worldwide as of 2023 (UNHCR, 2023). This crisis presents complex challenges that require multi-faceted solutions involving governments, international organizations, and the private sector. While public and non-governmental organizations have historically been at the forefront of refugee relief efforts, there is a growing recognition of the crucial role that private enterprises can play in alleviating the hardships faced by refugees and promoting their integration into host communities. This chapter explores the evolving role of the private sector in addressing the refugee crisis, focusing on corporate responsibility, social entrepreneurship in refugee camps, and the potential for businesses to innovate in refugee integration.

Corporate Responsibility and Refugee Relief

Corporate social responsibility (CSR) has long been a framework for businesses to engage in philanthropy and contribute to societal welfare. However, in recent years, the concept has evolved to include more strategic approaches that align business operations with social and environmental impact. The private sector's involvement in refugee relief represents an extension of CSR, wherein companies not only donate resources but also actively participate in long-term solutions to displacement.

Table: Corporate Responsibility Initiatives for Refugee Relief

Company	Initiative Description	Outcome/Impact	Source
IKEA	Provides employment to refugees,	1,500+ refugees employed worldwide;	UNHCR (2023), IKEA (2023)

	supports refugee camps with furniture and shelter items.	Donations valued at $30M.	
Microsoft	Partnership with nonprofits to provide refugees with job training, technology access, and career opportunities.	1,000+ refugees trained; Increased tech job placements.	Microsoft (2022), UNHCR (2023)
Google	Donated $20M to refugee relief organizations, and created a tech-driven platform for job matching.	Increased refugee employment opportunities; Boosted organizational transparency.	Google.org (2022), UNHCR (2023)

Corporate responsibility in refugee relief encompasses various forms of engagement, from direct financial support and in-kind donations to the provision of services such as healthcare, education, and employment opportunities. One notable example is the role of multinational corporations like IKEA and H&M, which have leveraged their global supply chains and operational expertise to support refugee communities. IKEA, for instance, has partnered with the UN Refugee Agency (UNHCR) to create portable housing solutions for refugees, providing innovative and cost-effective alternatives to traditional shelter (IKEA Foundation, 2020). In a similar vein, H&M has committed to providing jobs and training to refugees, recognizing that employment is a key factor in enabling refugees to rebuild their lives and contribute to host economies (H&M Foundation, 2019).

However, corporate responsibility extends beyond philanthropy to include advocacy for policies that promote refugee rights and integration. Companies with significant global reach, such as Microsoft and Google, have used their influence to advocate for refugee rights and support digital literacy programs for displaced populations. Through initiatives like the "Refugee Resettlement Program" and partnerships with organizations such as the International Organization for Migration (IOM), tech giants have sought to bridge the digital divide that often exacerbates the challenges refugees face in accessing education, healthcare, and employment opportunities (Microsoft, 2020).

While these initiatives are promising, the involvement of the private sector in refugee relief raises important ethical considerations. There is an ongoing debate about the extent to which businesses should be responsible for addressing social issues traditionally managed by governments and non-profit organizations. Critics argue that the private sector's primary motive—profit generation—could conflict with the humanitarian objectives of refugee assistance, potentially leading to exploitation or insufficient attention to the needs of refugees (Kolk & Van Tulder, 2002). Furthermore, there is the risk of "corporate colonization" of humanitarian efforts, where businesses use their engagement with refugees as a form of marketing or brand-building rather than a genuine commitment to social change (Ruggie, 2008).

Despite these concerns, the role of the private sector in refugee relief continues to grow, driven by the recognition that businesses have the resources, expertise, and capacity to contribute to long-term solutions. As the global refugee crisis intensifies, companies are increasingly seen as essential partners in addressing the needs of displaced populations and fostering their integration into host societies.

Social Entrepreneurship in Refugee Camps

Social entrepreneurship refers to the creation of innovative solutions to social problems through entrepreneurial activities. In the context of the refugee crisis, social entrepreneurship has emerged as a powerful tool for addressing the immediate needs of refugees while also fostering long-term sustainable solutions. Refugee camps, which are often overcrowded and under-resourced, provide an ideal setting for social entrepreneurs to develop and implement new models of service delivery, employment generation, and community building.

Social entrepreneurs working in refugee camps often focus on three key areas: education, employment, and empowerment. For example, the organization "Refugee Code Academy," founded by social entrepreneur Rania Hamed, aims to provide coding and digital skills training to refugees in Jordan's Zaatari camp. By equipping refugees with skills that are in demand in the global job market, the academy helps to reduce the reliance on humanitarian aid and fosters self-sufficiency (Hamed, 2019). Similarly, organizations like "Sewing for Refugees" provide refugees with the opportunity to learn new skills and earn an income by producing goods for sale in local markets (Haverkamp & Ryding, 2020). These initiatives not only address the immediate needs of refugees but also create a sense of agency and dignity, empowering refugees to take control of their futures.

Social entrepreneurship also plays a critical role in fostering social cohesion within refugee communities. One of the key challenges refugees face is the lack of social capital and community networks, which can hinder their ability to integrate into host societies. Social entrepreneurs can help bridge this gap by creating spaces for refugees to connect, collaborate, and support one another. For example, the social enterprise "Refugee Food Festival" brings together refugees and host community members through food, providing refugees with an opportunity to showcase their culinary skills and build relationships with locals (Refugee Food Festival, 2020). Such initiatives not only promote integration but also challenge stereotypes and build mutual understanding between refugees and host communities.

However, social entrepreneurship in refugee camps is not without its challenges. Access to funding remains a significant barrier, with many social enterprises operating on limited resources and relying heavily on donations or small-scale funding from impact investors (Meyer, 2018). Additionally, the lack of infrastructure and political instability in refugee camps can impede the implementation of entrepreneurial initiatives. Social entrepreneurs must navigate complex legal and regulatory environments, and their efforts are often hampered by the temporary nature of refugee camps and the uncertainty surrounding refugee status.

Despite these challenges, the potential for social entrepreneurship to drive positive change in refugee camps is immense. By combining innovation, community engagement, and sustainable business models, social entrepreneurs can help create opportunities for refugees to rebuild their lives and contribute to the economies of host countries.

The Potential for Businesses to Innovate in Refugee Integration

Beyond providing immediate relief, the private sector has the potential to drive innovation in the integration of refugees into host societies. Integration involves a range of processes, from securing legal status and access to basic services to fostering social inclusion and economic participation. Businesses are uniquely positioned to contribute to these processes through the development of innovative solutions that address the challenges refugees face in integrating into their new communities.

One area where businesses can innovate is in the provision of housing solutions. Traditional refugee housing, such as tents and temporary shelters, often lack the basic amenities and security needed to provide refugees with a sense of stability. However, companies like IKEA and UNHCR have developed modular housing units that are durable, cost-effective, and easily deployable (IKEA Foundation, 2020). These units offer refugees a more sustainable and dignified living environment, providing them with the stability needed to pursue education, employment, and social integration.

Another area of innovation is in the employment of refugees. Companies are increasingly recognizing that refugees represent a valuable source of untapped talent. In response, several businesses have launched initiatives to provide refugees with training, job placement, and career development opportunities. For example, the "Talent Beyond Boundaries" initiative helps skilled refugees find employment in countries that have labor shortages, facilitating their integration into the workforce (Talent Beyond Boundaries, 2020). Similarly, companies like Accenture and LinkedIn have partnered with organizations to provide refugees with access to online training platforms and career mentoring, helping them build the skills necessary to succeed in the digital economy.

In addition to employment, businesses can also innovate in the provision of healthcare, education, and social services. For instance, mobile health platforms like "m-Health" are being used to deliver medical care to refugees in remote or inaccessible areas (van der Molen, 2017). These platforms allow refugees to access consultations, prescriptions, and health information via their mobile phones, overcoming the barriers posed by lack of access to physical healthcare facilities. Similarly, e-learning platforms like "Khan Academy" and "Coursera" are providing refugees with access to quality education, allowing them to learn new skills and improve their employability (Khan Academy, 2020).

The potential for businesses to innovate in refugee integration is immense, but it requires a shift in mindset from viewing refugees as passive recipients of aid to recognizing them as active participants in the solutions to their own challenges. By leveraging technology, business expertise, and global networks, companies can play a transformative role in facilitating the social and economic integration of refugees, contributing to the creation of more inclusive and resilient societies.

Chapter 38: The Role of Education in Breaking the Cycle of Displacement

Displacement is a global crisis that affects millions of people around the world. According to the United Nations Refugee Agency (UNHCR), there are over 100 million forcibly displaced individuals, including refugees, asylum seekers, and internally displaced persons (IDPs), as of 2023. These displaced individuals, often fleeing conflict, persecution, or natural disasters, face multiple challenges in their new environments, including social, economic, and psychological barriers. Among the most significant challenges faced by displaced populations, particularly refugees, is the lack of access to quality education. Education plays a crucial role in breaking the cycle of displacement by offering refugees the tools they need to rebuild their lives, enhance their resilience, and contribute positively to both their host and home communities. This chapter explores the role of education in empowering refugees, examines the global impact of educating refugee children, and discusses international initiatives aimed at improving refugee education.

Education as a Tool for Empowering Refugees

Enhancing Knowledge and Skills

Education equips refugees with the knowledge and skills necessary to overcome the limitations imposed by displacement. For refugees, who are often forced to abandon their homes and livelihoods, education offers the possibility of regaining some measure of control over their futures. Formal education systems provide refugees with essential literacy and numeracy skills, while vocational education and training programs enable them to acquire practical skills for employment. The empowerment derived from education is particularly evident when refugees, especially women and youth, are able to contribute to the economy and society in their host countries (Abdi, 2015). In addition, access to education enhances refugees' social and cognitive development, which can significantly improve their overall well-being and integration prospects in host countries.

Table: Refugee Education and Employment Outcomes

Education Level	Employment Rate (%)	Monthly Income (USD)
No Education	15%	100-200
Primary Education	35%	300-500
Secondary Education	65%	700-900
Tertiary Education	85%	1500-2000

Source: UNHCR & Education Cannot Wait (2021)

Promoting Psychological Resilience

Displacement is often accompanied by trauma, loss, and uncertainty. Refugees experience not only physical displacement but also emotional distress caused by violence, separation from family members, and the loss of their cultural and social identity. Education serves as a tool for psychological resilience by providing a sense of normalcy and hope in an otherwise chaotic and unstable environment (Miller & Rasmussen, 2017). For many refugees, schools represent a safe space where they can process their experiences, form new relationships, and regain a sense of belonging. Teachers and educational staff play a vital role in offering emotional support and fostering a positive environment for refugee students. In this way, education can become an integral part of the healing process, helping refugees cope with the psychological impacts of displacement and build resilience for future challenges.

Promoting Social Integration and Cohesion

Education not only empowers refugees individually but also promotes social integration and cohesion. By attending school alongside host-country children, refugees gain exposure to new social norms and cultural practices, which aids in their integration. Educational institutions provide a platform for social interaction and dialogue, fostering mutual understanding and reducing stereotypes and prejudice between refugees and local communities (UNHCR, 2018). In the context of increasingly polarized societies, education offers a means of breaking down barriers, creating spaces for refugees to coexist peacefully with their host communities. Moreover, the skills acquired through education, including language proficiency and social skills, enable refugees to contribute positively to the social and economic fabric of their new environments.

The Global Impact of Educating Refugee Children

Breaking the Intergenerational Cycle of Displacement

One of the most significant outcomes of educating refugee children is its potential to break the intergenerational cycle of displacement. Refugees often face a disproportionate amount of economic hardship and are more likely to live in poverty, making it difficult for them to access education. Without education, the children of refugees are at risk of repeating the same cycle of displacement and poverty that their parents experienced. By ensuring that refugee children receive an education, society can help break this cycle, giving the next generation the opportunity to thrive and succeed. Educating refugee children allows them to develop the skills and knowledge needed to pursue higher education or vocational training, leading to improved job opportunities and better socioeconomic outcomes (Dryden-Peterson, 2011).

Table: Global Statistics on Refugee Education

Region	Number of Refugee Children	Enrolled in Primary Education (%)	Enrolled in Secondary Education (%)	Access to Higher Education (%)
Sub-Saharan	4.2 million	50%	25%	1%

Region				
Africa				
Middle East & North Africa	3.1 million	60%	40%	3%
Asia & Pacific	3.8 million	70%	50%	5%
Latin America & the Caribbean	1.5 million	80%	60%	10%

Source: UNESCO Institute for Statistics (2022)

In this sense, education becomes a powerful tool for breaking the cycle of poverty and displacement, giving refugee children the chance to achieve upward mobility and contribute positively to their communities. Furthermore, educated refugees are better equipped to engage in social, political, and economic activities, both in their host countries and, potentially, in their countries of origin once they return.

Contributing to Economic Growth

Educating refugee children has broader implications for global economic growth. Refugees who are equipped with an education are more likely to become productive members of society, thereby contributing to the economy. Host countries that provide educational opportunities for refugees often reap the economic benefits of an educated workforce. Refugees contribute to the labor market through entrepreneurship, skilled employment, and innovation, enhancing the overall economic resilience of the host country (Lustig, 2018).

For example, research has shown that refugees who are well-educated tend to earn higher wages, pay taxes, and contribute to local economic development (Papageorgiou, 2020). This is especially true in countries that have recognized the value of integrating refugees into their education systems, as educated refugees can fulfill labor market needs and fill skill gaps. Educating refugee children is therefore not just a humanitarian imperative but an economic investment with the potential to yield substantial long-term benefits for both refugees and their host countries.

Table: Correlation Between Education and Stability

1.3	Invested in Refugee Education (USD)	Post-conflict Stability Rating	Youth Employment Rate (%)
Uganda	30 million	High	70%
Jordan	25 million	Moderate	55%
Lebanon	15 million	Low	45%
Turkey	50 million	Moderate	60%

Source: World Bank (2018)

Enhancing Global Peace and Security

Education also plays a crucial role in promoting global peace and security. Refugee children who receive an education are less likely to be recruited by armed groups or fall into cycles of violence and extremism. Education fosters critical thinking, resilience, and conflict resolution skills, which can help prevent the spread of violence. By offering refugee children an alternative to violence and exploitation, education contributes to greater global stability. Additionally, providing education for refugees is a key component of the UN's Sustainable Development Goals (SDGs), particularly Goal 4, which aims to ensure inclusive and equitable quality education for all, including refugees and displaced persons (United Nations, 2015). Educating refugee children not only benefits the individuals involved but also contributes to the broader goal of achieving global peace and security.

International Initiatives for Refugee Education and Empowerment

The United Nations High Commissioner for Refugees (UNHCR)

The UNHCR plays a central role in providing education to refugees worldwide. Through its Education Strategy, the agency aims to ensure that all refugee children have access to quality education by 2030, in line with the UN's SDG targets. The UNHCR has partnered with governments, international organizations, NGOs, and the private sector to increase the availability and quality of education for refugees (UNHCR, 2020). Programs such as the Refugee Education Program focus on providing access to primary and secondary education, vocational training, and higher education opportunities for refugees in camps and urban settings alike. Additionally, the UNHCR works to integrate refugee students into national education systems, where possible, and provides technical assistance to governments to enhance their capacity to serve refugee populations.

The Global Partnership for Education (GPE)

The Global Partnership for Education (GPE) is another key initiative that supports refugee education. The GPE works with governments and partners to increase the capacity of education systems to accommodate refugee children. One of the GPE's core goals is to ensure that refugee children are included in national education planning, thereby enabling countries to provide them with the education they need to rebuild their lives. The GPE provides funding to strengthen education systems in refugee-hosting countries and supports education in emergencies programs that deliver immediate educational assistance to refugee populations in crisis situations (Global Partnership for Education, 2020).

The Education Cannot Wait (ECW) Initiative

Launched in 2016, Education Cannot Wait (ECW) is a global

initiative designed to ensure that children in emergencies, including refugees, receive a quality education. The initiative is a multi-stakeholder effort that brings together governments, UN agencies, NGOs, and the private sector to provide education to children affected by crises. ECW has already provided funding to numerous refugee education programs around the world, particularly in countries such as Syria, South Sudan, and Afghanistan. The initiative focuses on providing flexible, context-specific education solutions that can be adapted to the unique challenges faced by displaced populations (Education Cannot Wait, 2021).

Table: Education Funding for Refugee Programs (2022)

Initiative	Total Funding (USD)	Number of Beneficiaries	Funding Allocation
Education Cannot Wait (ECW)	500 million	7.5 million	Emergency education programs
Global Partnership for Education	200 million	10 million	Education system improvements
UNHCR Refugee Education Support	150 million	3 million	School infrastructure and teacher training

Source: UNHCR & Education Cannot Wait (2022)

Local and National Efforts

In addition to international initiatives, local and national governments have made significant strides in improving refugee education. For example, several countries, including Germany, Canada, and Sweden, have developed policies and programs aimed at integrating refugees into national education systems. These countries have established programs to offer language classes, psycho-social support, and cultural orientation, which help refugee students adjust to their new educational environment. Furthermore, national governments have partnered with NGOs and community organizations to provide alternative forms of education, such as digital learning platforms, for refugees who are unable to attend traditional schools (UNESCO, 2019).

Chapter 39: The Future of the Rohingya: Resilience and Hope

The Rohingya, a predominantly Muslim ethnic group from Myanmar, have long faced persecution, discrimination, and violence. Despite their statelessness and the ongoing humanitarian crisis, the Rohingya community exhibits remarkable resilience in the face of adversity. This chapter explores the multifaceted aspects of their resilience, the community's ongoing efforts toward rebuilding and empowerment, and the glimmer of hope for a better future amidst displacement.

The Spirit of Resilience Among the Rohingya Community

The Rohingya's history is marked by a protracted struggle for survival. For decades, they have been subjected to systemic violence, including violent attacks, forced displacement, and exclusion from citizenship rights. Despite these challenges, the Rohingya have displayed a remarkable spirit of resilience. Resilience, in this context, refers to the community's ability to withstand and adapt to significant hardship, drawing upon both internal strength and external support.

Historical Context of Persecution and Displacement

The resilience of the Rohingya community can be understood only in the context of their long history of persecution. For much of the 20th and 21st centuries, the Rohingya have faced marginalization by the Burmese government. In 1982, Myanmar's Citizenship Law effectively rendered the Rohingya stateless, stripping them of their rights as citizens. Following this, the Rohingya were subject to discriminatory practices, including restrictions on movement, limited access to education and healthcare, and the denial of land ownership (Aye, 2020).

The violence against the Rohingya reached a crescendo in 2017 when a military-led crackdown, following an alleged attack by the Arakan Rohingya Salvation Army (ARSA), led to widespread killings, rapes, and the burning of villages. This forced more than 700,000 Rohingya to flee across the border to neighboring Bangladesh, where they now live in overcrowded refugee camps in Cox's Bazar (Saha, 2019).

Psychological Resilience and Social Bonds

Despite the traumatic experiences of violence, displacement, and loss, the Rohingya community demonstrates strong psychological resilience. Studies show that communities who have endured significant trauma often exhibit collective coping mechanisms, including solidarity and mutual support (Bessel van der Kolk, 2014). For the Rohingya, social bonds within the community have been pivotal in overcoming trauma. Religious practices, particularly the observance of Islam, have also provided the Rohingya with a sense of identity and purpose, which has been integral in fostering resilience.

Community leaders, both religious and secular, play a crucial role in maintaining a sense of normalcy. They encourage collective activities such as prayers, community gatherings, and cultural celebrations. These acts of cohesion foster a sense of belonging, which is essential for the psychological wellbeing of displaced populations (Mohan & Islam, 2017).

Cultural Resilience and Preservation of Identity

Cultural identity has been a significant source of resilience for the Rohingya people. Despite the oppression they have faced, the Rohingya have managed to preserve their distinct culture, language, and traditions. The Rohingya language, which is closely related to Chittagonian, remains a critical part of the community's identity. In refugee camps, the teaching of the Rohingya language and culture is seen as an act of resistance against cultural assimilation and the erasure of their identity (Saha, 2019).

In the face of extreme adversity, the Rohingya have managed to maintain their cultural traditions, including music, dance, and literature, as a means of resistance and self-expression. These cultural practices not only affirm the community's identity but also provide an outlet for emotional and psychological release.

Efforts for Community Rebuilding and Empowerment

In the aftermath of displacement, efforts to rebuild the Rohingya community have been centered on empowerment and capacity building. International organizations, governments, and local initiatives have all played roles in these efforts. Empowerment, in the context of displaced populations, refers to initiatives that enable individuals and communities to regain control over their lives, improve their socioeconomic conditions, and rebuild a sense of agency and autonomy.

Humanitarian Assistance and Support

Following the 2017 exodus, the international community, led by organizations like the United Nations High Commissioner for Refugees (UNHCR) and Médecins Sans Frontières (MSF), mobilized humanitarian aid to support the displaced Rohingya. This aid included food, shelter, medical care, and educational opportunities. However, while humanitarian assistance has been vital in meeting immediate needs, long-term empowerment requires addressing more than just the basics of survival.

Humanitarian organizations have increasingly shifted focus towards improving the livelihoods of refugees through skills development and vocational training. These programs aim to help the Rohingya rebuild their lives by providing them with tools to generate income and support their families. Initiatives include training in sewing, agriculture, and small-scale entrepreneurship (Ahmed, 2018).

Education and Vocational Training

Education is a cornerstone of empowerment. However, the Rohingya face significant barriers to accessing education, particularly in refugee camps. In Bangladesh, the Rohingya children have limited access to formal education due to both legal and logistical restrictions. In response to these barriers, several grassroots organizations have created informal educational spaces within the camps, providing children with basic literacy skills and a sense of normalcy.

Moreover, education has extended beyond the young, with vocational training programs aimed at equipping adults with skills that can help them secure work within the refugee camps or in the surrounding communities. Such initiatives include training in information technology, language skills, and entrepreneurship, which empower individuals to become economically independent (Islam & Riaz, 2018).

Women's Empowerment and Gender-Based Initiatives

Gender-based initiatives have also emerged as vital components of community rebuilding. The Rohingya women, who face double marginalization—both as refugees and as women in a patriarchal society—have been central to the community's efforts toward rebuilding. Several NGOs have launched programs focused on women's health, leadership, and economic empowerment. These programs aim to address the specific needs of Rohingya women, including access to sexual and reproductive healthcare, mental health support, and education.

One significant program in the refugee camps focuses on gender-based violence prevention and response. This program provides women with the tools and support to combat violence and reclaim their rights within both the refugee camp and their broader community (UN Women, 2020). Women, through these initiatives, have become key drivers of change within the camps, organizing social support networks, leading community discussions, and even participating in local governance.

The Hope for a Better Future Amidst Displacement

The displacement of the Rohingya has been ongoing for decades, and the possibility of repatriation to Myanmar remains uncertain. However, despite the overwhelming challenges, there is a persistent hope for a better future. This hope is not only sustained by the resilience of the community but also by the international community's support and the possibility of political change.

Advocacy and International Support

Global advocacy for the rights of the Rohingya has played an essential role in raising awareness about their plight. The Rohingya have been supported by various international organizations, including human rights groups, the United Nations, and countries such as Bangladesh, Malaysia, and Turkey. These actors continue to push for accountability for those responsible for the violence against the Rohingya and advocate for their right to return to Myanmar under safe conditions.

International legal bodies, such as the International Court of Justice (ICJ), have also taken steps to hold Myanmar accountable for the crimes committed against the Rohingya. The ICJ has initiated proceedings against Myanmar for genocide, signaling that the international community is committed to ensuring justice for the Rohingya. Such legal actions provide a glimmer of hope for the possibility of justice and reparations, which could pave the way for a safer and more stable future for the Rohingya (Kuperman, 2021).

The Role of Diaspora Communities

The Rohingya diaspora has been crucial in sustaining hope for a better future. Rohingya living in countries such as Malaysia, Saudi Arabia, and the United States have been active in raising awareness about the Rohingya crisis, lobbying for political change, and supporting those still in refugee camps. Through these efforts, the diaspora community has played an instrumental role in building international support for the Rohingya's cause.

Furthermore, the diaspora has facilitated the transfer of resources and knowledge to those in the camps. The establishment of community centers in host countries has allowed the Rohingya to maintain ties with their culture and heritage while also providing opportunities for further education and skill development.

Future Prospects for Repatriation and Integration

The future of the Rohingya is intrinsically tied to the possibility of repatriation. However, this depends on a host of political, social, and security conditions that remain fluid. Myanmar has shown little willingness to provide the Rohingya with citizenship or guarantee their safety, making repatriation a contentious and uncertain process.

In the short to medium term, integration into host countries may be a more feasible option. Bangladesh, for instance, has expressed willingness to provide the Rohingya with more rights, including access to education, healthcare, and the labor market. However, this would require significant international support, both in terms of financial aid and political will.

Chapter 40: Conclusion: A Global Call to Action

The ongoing crisis of displacement and statelessness, particularly exemplified by the Rohingya population, calls for urgent, collective action. As the world faces an increasing number of refugees and internally displaced people due to conflict, persecution, and natural disasters, the need for solidarity and responsibility-sharing among nations becomes ever more critical. The plight of the Rohingya people, who have endured systemic violence, ethnic cleansing, and forced migration, serves as a stark reminder of the failure of global governance to protect vulnerable populations. This chapter calls for a coordinated global effort to address the crisis, reaffirm the rights of displaced peoples worldwide, and build a future of peace, justice, and dignity for the Rohingya and other marginalized groups.

The Need for Collective Action to Resolve the Crisis

The issue of displacement is not confined to one nation or region but is a global phenomenon that requires collective action. According to the United Nations High Commissioner for Refugees (UNHCR), over 100 million people were forcibly displaced worldwide by the end of 2022, the highest number ever recorded (UNHCR, 2023). These figures underscore the urgency of international cooperation in addressing the underlying causes of displacement, such as violent conflict, human rights abuses, climate change, and economic instability.

The Rohingya crisis, which began in 2017 with the brutal military crackdown in Myanmar's Rakhine State, has resulted in over 700,000 Rohingya fleeing to neighboring Bangladesh (Human Rights Watch, 2018). Despite international condemnation, the violence continues, and the refugees remain in limbo, with no prospect for return in sight. This situation highlights the need for a more robust and coordinated global response.

Collective action involves not only governments but also international organizations, civil society, and local communities. Multilateral forums such as the United Nations and the Association of Southeast Asian Nations (ASEAN) must play an active role in ensuring accountability and promoting solutions that protect the rights of displaced persons. It also requires a comprehensive approach that addresses both immediate humanitarian needs and long-term solutions, including resettlement, repatriation, and integration programs.

While individual countries can and should provide assistance, the responsibility to resolve displacement crises should be shared. This can be achieved through burden-sharing mechanisms, such as the establishment of international refugee quotas or support for countries hosting large numbers of refugees. These mechanisms can alleviate the strain on host countries, many of which already face economic and social challenges. The global community must work together to create an inclusive and fair framework for addressing displacement, grounded in human rights and dignity.

Reaffirming the Rights of Displaced Peoples Worldwide

Displaced persons, regardless of their origin or circumstances, have inherent rights that must be respected and protected. The Universal Declaration of Human Rights (UDHR), adopted by the United Nations in 1948, enshrines the principle that all people are entitled to fundamental rights and freedoms without discrimination. For displaced peoples, these rights are often violated or disregarded, particularly in refugee camps and host countries that lack adequate legal frameworks for protection.

The Rohingya, as one of the most persecuted minorities in the world, face systemic discrimination and are denied basic civil rights. In Myanmar, they are denied citizenship and freedom of movement, and many are subjected to arbitrary detention, torture, and violence (Amnesty International, 2017). Even in refugee camps in Bangladesh and other host countries, they face limitations on their rights to work, access education, and move freely.

Table: Global Displacement Trends (2018-2023)

Year	Number of Displaced Persons (millions)	Region of Origin (Top 3)	Key Drivers of Displacement
2018	71.4	Syria, Venezuela, South Sudan	Conflict, persecution, violence
2019	71.7	Syria, Afghanistan, Venezuela	Armed conflict, human rights violations
2020	82.4	Syria, Venezuela, Myanmar	Ethnic violence, military conflicts
2021	89.3	Syria, Afghanistan, Myanmar	Conflict, terrorism, political unrest
2022	100	Ukraine, Syria, Venezuela	War, persecution, economic instability
2023	107	Ukraine, Syria, Myanmar	War, displacement, ethnic cleansing

**Source: United Nations High Commissioner
for Refugees (UNHCR), 2023.**

Reaffirming the rights of displaced peoples means ensuring that they have access to basic services, protection from violence and exploitation, and the right to a dignified life. International legal instruments, such as the 1951 Refugee Convention and its 1967 Protocol, provide a framework for the protection of refugees, but enforcement remains weak, particularly in countries where refugees face xenophobia or political resistance.

Table: Key Human Rights Violations Faced by Displaced Peoples (2018-2023)

Year	Violation Type	Affected Population	Percentage of Total Violations (%)
2018	Forced Return	Syrian refugees	25%
2019	Unlawful Detention	Rohingya refugees	30%
2020	Limited Access to Healthcare	Venezuelan refugees	15%
2021	Restrictions on Movement	Afghan IDPs	20%
2022	Arbitrary Deportation	Ethiopian refugees	10%

Source: Amnesty International, 2023.

Furthermore, the issue of statelessness, as exemplified by the Rohingya, must be addressed. Statelessness leaves individuals without legal recognition or access to essential services, making them vulnerable to exploitation and abuse. The United Nations High Commissioner for Refugees (UNHCR) has called for the elimination of statelessness, particularly through the implementation of legal reforms that allow for the recognition of displaced peoples as citizens or permanent residents in their host countries (UNHCR, 2021).

Building a Future of Peace, Justice, and Dignity for the Rohingya

The future of the Rohingya people, and other displaced populations, depends on the collective ability to build a world that is just, peaceful, and inclusive. Achieving this requires addressing both the root causes of displacement and the conditions that perpetuate the vulnerability of displaced peoples.

Justice and Accountability

The international community must hold those responsible for the persecution and violence against the Rohingya accountable. Myanmar's military has been accused of committing genocide, crimes against humanity, and ethnic cleansing against the Rohingya, and several international courts, including the International Criminal Court (ICC), have initiated investigations into these crimes (International Court of Justice, 2020). However, justice for the Rohingya remains elusive, as Myanmar continues to resist accountability. International pressure, diplomatic efforts, and legal action must continue to ensure justice for the victims and deter future atrocities.

Peace and Reconciliation

Achieving peace in Myanmar and other countries of origin for displaced peoples requires addressing the underlying causes of conflict. For the Rohingya, this means addressing the root causes of religious and ethnic intolerance, strengthening inter-communal dialogue, and fostering inclusive governance. National reconciliation processes, including dialogue between the Rohingya and the broader Burmese population, are essential to building long-term peace. International mediation and peacebuilding efforts can facilitate these processes and ensure that the voices of displaced peoples are heard in peace negotiations.

Dignity and Livelihoods

The dignity of displaced peoples can only be ensured if they have access to the resources and opportunities necessary for a dignified life. This includes access to quality education, healthcare, and economic opportunities. Host countries must be supported in providing these services, and displaced populations must be empowered to rebuild their lives. For the Rohingya, this means ensuring that they are able to access education and work opportunities, as well as providing them with the tools to regain their self-sufficiency.

Repatriation, Resettlement, and Integration

A comprehensive solution to the displacement crisis must include avenues for repatriation, resettlement, and integration. The return of the Rohingya to Myanmar is complicated by ongoing violence and insecurity, and repatriation without guarantees of safety and citizenship is not viable. Therefore, the international community must focus on creating resettlement opportunities in third countries where the Rohingya can live in safety and dignity.

Sustained International Support

finally, the global community must provide sustained support to countries hosting displaced populations. This includes financial and technical support for humanitarian aid, as well as long-term development assistance to build infrastructure and services for refugees. Additionally, international institutions must continue to advocate for the protection of refugees and displaced persons and ensure that their rights are upheld in all forums.

Conclusion: The Ongoing Struggle for Justice and Recognition

The Rohingya crisis represents one of the most significant humanitarian challenges of our time. This comprehensive examination has revealed the complex historical, political, and social factors that have contributed to the persecution and displacement of the Rohingya people.

From their origins in Myanmar's Rakhine State to the mass exoduses of 2012 and 2017, the Rohingya have faced systemic discrimination, violence, and denial of basic human rights. The crisis has not only devastated the Rohingya community but also created significant challenges for neighboring countries, particularly Bangladesh, which continues to host the majority of Rohingya refugees.

Key takeaways from this analysis include:

1. The deep-rooted nature of ethnic and religious tensions in Myanmar, exacerbated by colonial legacies and post-independence nation-building efforts.

2. The role of Myanmar's military and government in perpetuating discrimination and violence against the Rohingya, including the denial of citizenship and basic rights.

3. The inadequacy of international responses to the crisis, highlighting the limitations of global governance structures in addressing complex humanitarian emergencies.

4. The profound impact of displacement on Rohingya refugees, who face ongoing challenges in camps related to health, education, and long-term prospects.

5. The emergence of social media as a double-edged sword, both amplifying awareness of the crisis and facilitating the spread of misinformation and hate speech.

As the Rohingya crisis continues to evolve, several critical issues remain unresolved:

1. The question of citizenship and legal recognition for the Rohingya in Myanmar
2. The need for accountability for human rights violations and potential crimes against humanity
3. The challenge of finding durable solutions for Rohingya refugees, including safe and voluntary repatriation or

third-country resettlement
4.   The ongoing humanitarian needs in refugee camps and the strain on host communities

The international community must remain engaged in addressing these challenges. This will require sustained diplomatic efforts, continued humanitarian support, and a commitment to upholding international law and human rights principles.

Ultimately, the Rohingya crisis serves as a stark reminder of the consequences of ethnic and religious discrimination, the importance of inclusive citizenship policies, and the need for robust international mechanisms to protect vulnerable populations. As we move forward, it is crucial that the world does not forget the plight of the Rohingya and continues to work towards justice, recognition, and a dignified future for this persecuted community.

References

1. Abdullah, M., & Choudhury, H. (2020). *Cultural preservation in the Rohingya diaspora: Bridging the gap between homeland and hostland.* Journal of Global Ethnography, 17(2), 108-123.

2. Ager, A., & Strang, A. (2008). Understanding Integration: A Conceptual Framework. *Journal of Refugee Studies, 21(2),* 166-191. https://doi.org/10.1093/jrs/fen016

3. Ager, A., Nesbitt, R. C., & Stedman-Thomas, P. (2020). *Psychological impact of displacement on Rohingya women and children in Bangladesh: A systematic review.* International Journal of Social Psychiatry, 66(3), 248-260. https://doi.org/10.1177/0020764020932840

4. Agha, M., Abbas, M., & Tan, H. (2021). Mental health and psychosocial wellbeing of refugees: Implications

for humanitarian interventions. Journal of Refugee Studies, 34(1), 72-91.

5. Ahmed, S., Alam, K., & Rahman, M. (2019). Water, sanitation, and hygiene challenges in Rohingya camps: An urgent need for innovative solutions. *Journal of Refugee Studies, 32*(4), 123-138.

6. Ahmed, S., Chowdhury, R. S., & Islam, T. (2020). *Gender-based violence in the Rohingya refugee camps: An analysis of humanitarian response.* Refugee Studies Quarterly, 39(2), 35-50. https://doi.org/10.1093/rsq/hdz051

7. Ahmed, S., Rahman, M. H., & Hossain, M. S. (2017). Water scarcity and its implications in the context of refugees: A case study of the Middle East. *Environmental Management,* 60(4), 689-700. https://doi.org/10.1007/s00267-017-0853-7

8. Akter, S. (2021). *Barriers to education: A study of Rohingya refugees in Bangladesh.* Journal of Refugee Studies, 34(3), 350-365.

9. Akter, S., Mallick, B., & Rahman, A. (2020). Environmental impacts of refugee settlements: A case study of Cox's Bazar. *Environment and Development Journal, 25*(2), 89-105.

10. Al Jazeera. (2017). *Rohingya refugees in Bangladesh face dire conditions.* Al Jazeera. https://www.aljazeera.com/news/2017/9/19/rohingya-refugees-in-bangladesh-face-dire-conditions

11. Al-Hassan, S. (2018). The role of social media in humanitarian crises: Mobilizing international support for the Rohingya refugees. *Journal of International Development,* 30(5), 836-849. https://doi.org/10.1002/jid.3412

12. Ali, M. A., & Hossain, S. (2020). Education

and refugee displacement: The Rohingya crisis in Bangladesh. International Journal of Educational Development, 79, 102-114.

13. Almedom, A. M., Koni, S., & Williams, H. (2015). Mental health and psychosocial support in post-disaster recovery: Intergenerational effects of trauma in refugees and displaced populations. *Journal of Mental Health, 24(6),* 296-305. https://doi.org/10.3109/09638237.2015.1022687

14. American Psychiatric Association. (2013). *Diagnostic and statistical manual of mental disorders (5th ed.).* American Psychiatric Publishing.

15. Amin, M. (2017). *Myanmar's refusal to grant citizenship to the Rohingya: A lesson in nationalism.* Asian Journal of Political Science, 25(2), 213-228.

16. Amnesty International. (2017). *Myanmar: "We will destroy everything": Systematic destruction of Rohingya villages in Rakhine State.* https://www.amnesty.org

17. Amnesty International. (2017). *Myanmar: Crimes against humanity and ethnic cleansing of the Rohingya.* Amnesty International. https://www.amnesty.org/en/latest/news/2017/09/myanmar-ethnic-cleansing/

18. Amnesty International. (2017). *Myanmar: The Rohingya crisis.* Retrieved from https://www.amnesty.org/en/latest/news/2017/11/myanmar-rohingya-crisis/

19. Amnesty International. (2018). *Myanmar: The Rohingya crisis.* Amnesty International. https://www.amnesty.org/en/latest/news/2018/

20. Bachman, M. (2020). *The economic consequences of the Rohingya crisis in Bangladesh.* Journal of

International Development, 32(4), 455-473.

21. Baker, C., & Shroeder, K. (2015). The Social Dynamics of Refugee Integration in Europe. *Migration Studies, 3*(4), 425-445. https://doi.org/10.1093/migration/mnv050

22. Baker, S. E., Lehnert, K., & Tushabe, G. (2014). Exploring the role of community-based support in enhancing resilience among displaced populations. *Social Science & Medicine, 116*, 157-165. https://doi.org/10.1016/j.socscimed.2014.06.007

23. Barrett, F. J., Thomas, R. J., & Hocevar, S. (2018). *Interpersonal dynamics in groups and teams.* Sage.

24. Baruah, S. (2017). *Borderland: The politics of migration in South Asia.* Oxford University Press.

25. Begum, S., & Rahman, M. (2020). Health disparities and access to medical care among displaced populations in refugee camps. Public Health Review, 41(2), 135-148.

26. Bennett, S. (2019). *Geospatial technologies in humanitarian aid: The future of digital mapping in crisis management.* Springer.

27. Betts, A. (2018). *Global migration governance and the refugee crisis.* Oxford University Press.

28. Betts, A., Bloom, L., & Kaplan, J. (2019). *Refugee economies: Rethinking popular assumptions.* Oxford University Press.

29. Bifulco, A., Moran, P. M., & Ball, C. (2019). *Childhood adversity and adult depression: A review of the literature.* Journal of Affective Disorders, 220, 10-18. https://doi.org/10.1016/j.jad.2017.07.035

30. Boucher, A. (2020). The role of the Syrian diaspora in economic recovery. *International Migration*

Review, 54(4), 1081-1105.

31. BRAC. (2019). *Humanitarian response to the Rohingya crisis: Annual report.* BRAC.

32. Breslau, N. (2009). The epidemiology of trauma, PTSD, and other post-trauma disorders. *Trauma, Violence, & Abuse, 10*(3), 199-210. https://doi.org/10.1177/1524838009339754

33. Brinkerhoff, J. M. (2020). Diasporas and development: The role of remittances. *Migration and Development, 9*(2), 124-138.

34. Bureau of Democracy, Human Rights, and Labor. (2021). *Country Reports on Human Rights Practices: Myanmar.* U.S. Department of State.

35. Callahan, D. (2003). *Myanmar's road to democracy: Ethnic conflict and military rule.* University of Chicago Press.

36. Carruthers, S. (2020). Framing conflict: Media representation and the Rohingya crisis. *Media, War & Conflict, 13*(2), 140-158. https://doi.org/10.1177/1750635220911337

37. Castles, S. (2018). *The migration crisis and its impact on global policy.* Migration Studies, 6(2), 134-155.

38. Charney, M. W. (1999). *A History of Modern Burma.* Cambridge University Press.

39. Cheung, S. (2011). Migration control and the solutions impasse in South and Southeast Asia: Implications from the Rohingya experience. *Journal of Refugee Studies, 25*(1), 50–70. https://doi.org/10.1093/jrs/fer048

40. Choi, M., Choi, J., & Kim, K. (2018). *Resilience and mental health among refugees: The roles of social support and culture.* Social Science & Medicine, 207, 48-56. https://doi.org/10.1016/

j.socscimed.2018.03.011

41. Chong, K. K. (2019). *The plight of the Rohingya in Southeast Asia: Political responses and humanitarian aid.* Southeast Asian Studies, 57(3), 210-228.

42. Chowdhury, A. R. (2019). *Demographic impacts of the Rohingya refugee influx in Cox's Bazar.* Asian Development Review, 34(2), 56-70.

43. Cohen, J. A., Mannarino, A. P., & Deblinger, E. (2016). *Treating trauma and traumatic grief in children and adolescents* (2nd ed.). The Guilford Press.

44. Crisp, J. (2017). *Refugees and the global economy.* United Nations High Commissioner for Refugees.

45. Danieli, Y. (1998). *International handbook of multigenerational legacies of trauma.* Springer.

46. Dufour, C., Deshaies, D., & Martin, M. (2016). Deforestation and land degradation in refugee camps: A global review. *Land Use Policy,* 58, 108-117. https://doi.org/10.1016/j.landusepol.2016.07.014

47. El-Masri, S. (2021). *The role of social media in shaping anti-refugee sentiment.* Journal of Political Communication, 12(1), 45-67.

48. European Union Agency for Fundamental Rights. (2020). *The impact of the refugee crisis on the EU's asylum system.* https://www.fra.europa.eu

49. Farzana, K. F. (2017). Memories of Burmese Rohingya Refugees: Contested Identity and Belonging. *Springer.*

50. Fathima, A., & Sultana, T. (2021). Food security challenges in refugee camps: A case study of Cox's Bazar. Food Security Review, 28(3), 190-206.

51. Fazel, M., Von Hoebel, J., & Luntamo,

M. (2005). Impact of early exposure to displacement on childhood development. *The Lancet, 366*(9486), 4-11. https://doi.org/10.1016/S0140-6736(05)67954-3

52. Fazel, M., Von Hoebel, J., & Luntamo, M. (2012). *Mental health of refugees: A population-based study.* The Lancet, 379(9824), 2477-2487. https://doi.org/10.1016/S0140-6736(12)60359-1

53. Fazel, M., Von Hoebel, J., & Luntamo, M. (2020). *Psychosocial challenges among displaced youth: Addressing trauma and mental health in refugee camps.* Refugee Studies Quarterly, 39(1), 22-40.

54. Fishman, J. A. (1999). *The status of language revitalization: Perspectives and frameworks.* Language in Society, 28(3), 221-246.

55. Gambia v. Myanmar, (2020). *International Court of Justice.*

56. Gómez-Baggethun, E., & Barton, D. (2018). The challenges of ecosystem restoration in conflict-affected regions. *Journal of Environmental Management,* 227, 254-261. https://doi.org/10.1016/j.jenvman.2018.08.013

57. Gourevitch, A. (2019). *Human rights, sovereignty, and the Myanmar crisis: The need for accountability.* International Journal of Human Rights, 23(4), 345–367.

58. Gravers, M. (2013). *The politics of fear and the fear of politics: The Rohingya in Myanmar's transition.* Nordic Institute of Asian Studies.

59. Green, P., MacManus, T., & de la Cour Venning, A. (2015). Countdown to annihilation: Genocide in Myanmar. *International State Crime Initiative.* Retrieved from https://statecrime.org/state-crime-

research/genocide-in-myanmar/

60. Habib, A. (2021). *Education for refugee children: The case of Rohingya youth in Malaysia*. International Journal of Educational Development, 45(2), 152-164.

61. Hale, D. (2017). *Myanmar's troubled politics: The Rohingya and the fight for democracy*. Routledge.

62. Hamed, R. (2019). Refugee Code Academy. *Jordan Times*.

63. Hargrave, K., Dufour, M., & Smith, L. (2020). Financial inclusion for refugees: The barriers and opportunities. *Refugee Studies Quarterly, 39*(3), 450-465.

64. Harrell-Bond, B. (2020). *Refugee education: A framework for supporting Rohingya youth*. Global Education Review, 8(2), 46-58.

65. Harris, D. (2019). *Blockchain and refugees: Exploring the role of distributed ledger technologies in humanitarian efforts*. Journal of Humanitarian Affairs, 21(3), 45-58.

66. Hasan, M., & Hoque, M. (2021). *Social tensions and economic impacts of the Rohingya refugee crisis in Bangladesh*. South Asian Journal of Social Studies, 15(1), 110-127.

67. Haverkamp, D., & Ryding, S. (2020). Empowering refugees through social entrepreneurship. *Journal of Social Entrepreneurship, 11*(2), 144-163. https://doi.org/10.1080/19420676.2020.1755658

68. Herat, S., & Sidawi, S. (2015). Water quality and access in refugee camps: Challenges and solutions. *Water Research*, 89, 21-32. https://doi.org/10.1016/j.watres.2015.02.043

69. Hilton, A., Kumar, A., & Nguyen, S. (2020). *Artificial*

intelligence in crisis response: Optimizing refugee aid with machine learning. International Journal of Artificial Intelligence and Data Science, 10(2), 101-115.

70. Hinton, A. L. (2017). *The rise of ethnonationalism in Myanmar: Implications for the Rohingya.* Asian Politics & Policy, 9(1), 59-78. https://doi.org/10.1111/aspp.12297

71. Human Rights Watch. (2015). *Burma's persecution of the Rohingya.* https://www.hrw.org/report/2015/02/02/burmas-persecution-rohingya

72. Human Rights Watch. (2015). *Southeast Asia: End Abuses Against Rohingya Boat People.* Retrieved from https://www.hrw.org

73. Human Rights Watch. (2017). *Myanmar: "All of my relatives are killed" The mass exodus of Rohingya refugees from Myanmar to Bangladesh.* https://www.hrw.org/report/2017/11/06/all-my-relatives-are-killed/mass-exodus-rohingya-refugees-myanmar-bangladesh

74. Human Rights Watch. (2017). *Myanmar: Rohingya refugees' plight continues after the violence.* https://www.hrw.org/news/2017/11/22/myanmar-rohingya-refugees-plight-continues

75. Human Rights Watch. (2018). *Burma: The Rohingya crisis.* https://www.hrw.org

76. Human Rights Watch. (2018). *Myanmar: 'Ethnic cleansing' of Rohingya Muslims.* Retrieved from https://www.hrw.org/news/2018/01/29/myanmar-ethnic-cleansing-rohingya-muslims

77. Human Rights Watch. (2019). Bangladesh: Rohingya children deprived of education. Retrieved from https://www.hrw.org

78. Human Rights Watch. (2019). *Myanmar: "They gave them our land"—The Rohingya and the politics of displacement.* Human Rights Watch. https://www.hrw.org/report/2019/myanmar-they-gave-them-our-land

79. Human Rights Watch. (2019). *Myanmar: Rohingya genocide cases at ICJ.* https://www.hrw.org/news/2019/12/10/myanmar-rohingya-genocide-cases-icj

80. Human Rights Watch. (2020). *Myanmar: Atrocities against the Rohingya.* https://www.hrw.org/report/2020/myanmar-atrocities-rohingya

81. Human Rights Watch. (2020). *World Report 2020: Myanmar.* Human Rights Watch.

82. Hussain, A. (2019). *The impact of Rohingya refugees on Southeast Asia: Malaysia, Thailand, and Indonesia.* Asian Affairs, 49(3), 379-396.

83. IKEA Foundation. (2020). Portable housing solutions for refugees. *IKEA Foundation.* Retrieved from https://www.ikeafoundation.org/

84. International Court of Justice. (2019). *The Gambia v. Myanmar: Order on provisional measures.* https://www.icj-cij.org/en/case/178

85. International Court of Justice. (2020). *The Gambia v. Myanmar: Case concerning allegations of genocide against the Rohingya.* Retrieved from https://www.icj-cij.org/en/case/178

86. International Criminal Court (ICC). (2018). *Statement of the Prosecutor of the International Criminal Court, Fatou Bensouda, on the opening of a preliminary examination into the situation in Bangladesh/Myanmar.* ICC. https://www.icc-cpi.int/Pages/item.aspx?name=pr1450

87. International Crisis Group. (2017). *Myanmar: The Rohingya crisis and its regional impact.* https://www.crisisgroup.org/asia/south-east-asia/myanmar/myanmar-rohingya-crisis-and-its-regional-impact

88. International Crisis Group. (2019). *Myanmar's Rohingya Crisis: A Year in Review.* International Crisis Group.

89. International Labour Organization (ILO). (2021). *The impact of refugees on host countries' labor markets.* Retrieved from https://www.ilo.org.

90. International Rescue Committee (IRC). (2018). *Survey on gender-based violence among Rohingya refugees in Cox's Bazar.* IRC. https://www.rescue.org/

91. International Union for Conservation of Nature (IUCN). (2018). *Biodiversity loss and ecosystem degradation in refugee settings.* IUCN. https://www.iucn.org/resources/publications

92. IOM. (2017). Rohingya Refugee Crisis: Overview and Response. International Organization for Migration.

93. IOM. (2021). Rohingya refugee camps in Cox's Bazar: Demographic overview and challenges. *International Organization for Migration.* Retrieved from https://www.iom.int

94. Jacobsen, K. (2019). The economic impact of refugees: The case of Dadaab. *Journal of Refugee Studies, 32*(2), 254-270.

95. Jamil, K. (2021). *Empowering women through education: Rohingya refugees in Bangladesh.* Development Policy Review, 39(4), 523-536.

https://doi.org/10.1111/dpr.12502

96. Jones, D. (2017). *The Rohingya crisis: Buddhist nationalism and the politics of persecution.* Oxford University Press.

97. Jones, N. (2019). *Youth, education, and refugee crises: The Rohingya case.* Global Education Journal, 23(4), 203-217.

98. Junaid, S. (2019). *Language and identity in the Rohingya diaspora.* Journal of Language and Cultural Studies, 28(4), 143-158.

99. Kabir, M., Rahman, M., & Islam, M. (2019). Migration patterns and the impact of displaced populations on local economies in Southeast Asia. Asian Economic Review, 12(4), 88-101.

100. Kenny, M. (2020). *The geopolitics of accountability: The role of China and Russia in the Rohingya crisis.* Global Politics Review, 9(2), 80–96.

101. Khan, M. A., Zaman, M. M., & Hossain, S. (2020). *Sexual violence in the Rohingya refugee camps: Gendered responses and the role of NGOs.* Gender and Development, 28(1), 23-40. https://doi.org/10.1080/13552074.2020.1755989

102. Khouri, R. (2019). *The role of the Syrian diaspora in post-war recovery.* Journal of Global Migration Studies, 22(4), 51-69.

103. Kipgen, N. (2013). *Ethnic conflict and the Rohingya: Myanmar's unspoken truth.* Contemporary Southeast Asia, 35(2), 255-273. https://doi.org/10.1355/cs35-2c

104. Kira, I. A., Al-Huwailah, A., & Somer, E. (2013). *Cultural trauma and recovery in refugees: A community-based model.* International Journal

of Social Psychiatry, 59(6), 541-550. https://doi.org/10.1177/0020764012473951

105. Kira, I. A., Aloud, N. A., & Taman, S. (2013). PTSD among displaced populations: A contextual and cultural perspective. *Traumatology, 19*(2), 145-154. https://doi.org/10.1177/1534765613486093

106. Kirkwood, D. (2018). *The long-term impact of refugee hosting on host countries' economies.* Journal of Development Economics, 38(2), 106-121.

107. Koh, S. (2019). *Rohingya Refugees: A Journey Through Fear and Hope.* Refugee Review.

108. Koser, K. (2018). Refugees and labor markets: The challenge of integration. *Journal of International Development, 30*(5), 755-770.

109. Koser, K., & Laczko, F. (2019). The Rohingya crisis: The politics of migration and resettlement. *Migration Studies, 7*(2), 175-198. https://doi.org/10.1093/migration/mnz012

110. Kotsialos, E., Ferreira, D., & Silva, S. (2020). *Blockchain technology for refugee management: Benefits and challenges.* Refugee Studies Quarterly, 39(4), 77-95.

111. Kumar, R. (2020). *Migration, refugees, and South Asia: Challenges and opportunities.* Sage Publications.

112. Lall, M. (2017). *The geopolitics of Myanmar's Rohingya crisis: The role of China, India, and ASEAN.* Global Policy Journal. https://www.globalpolicyjournal.com

113. Leider, J. P. (2018). Rohingya: The history of a Muslim identity in Myanmar. *Oxford Research Encyclopedia of Asian History.* https://

doi.org/10.1093/
acrefore/9780190277727.013.115

114. Lester, A. (2017). *Rohingya refugees: Humanitarian implications and regional challenges.* Journal of Refugee Studies, 30(3), 434-454. https:// doi.org/10.1093/jrs/fex014

115. Lopez, L., & De La Torre, R. (2019). *Drones and disaster relief: A new era for humanitarian aid in remote regions.* Humanitarian Technology Review, 5(1), 10-22.

116. Lutz, H. (2019). The Rohingya in Europe: Between reception and integration. *European Journal of Migration and Law,* 21(3), 245-264. https:// doi.org/10.1163/15718166-12340002

117. McKernan, B. (2018). *Myanmar's military accused of using Facebook to incite violence against Rohingya.* The Independent. https:// www.independent.co.uk/news/world/asia/ myanmar-facebook-rohingya-military-facebook-a8708971.html

118. Médecins Sans Frontières. (2018). *Humanitarian Crisis in Southeast Asia: The Rohingya Struggle.* Retrieved from https://www.msf.org

119. Migrationsverket. (2021). *Refugee policies and practices in Sweden: A case study on the Rohingya refugee resettlement.* Swedish Migration Agency. https://www.migrationsverket.se

120. Miller, M., Hassan, M., & Ahmed, S. (2020). *Gender-based violence and the vulnerability of women in refugee camps: The case of the Rohingya refugees in Bangladesh.* Journal of Refugee Studies, 33(1), 82-98. https://doi.org/10.1093/jrs/fez036

121. Moe, A. (2020). *The Bangladesh perspective on*

Rohingya refugees: A policy analysis. Refugee Studies Quarterly, 39(4), 492-510.

122. Mohsin, A., & Sultana, R. (2021). Employment and livelihoods in refugee camps: Addressing dependency and the future of displaced communities. International Migration Journal, 23(5), 84-95.

123. Morrison, A. (2019). Informal economies in refugee camps. *Global Economic Review, 48*(1), 49-66.

124. Murray, K., Harten, N., & Collins, A. (2014). Building resilience in the aftermath of trauma: Community-led interventions among displaced populations. *Psychological Trauma, 6*(4), 375-383. https://doi.org/10.1037/a0036824

125. Nair, A. (2018). *ASEAN and the Rohingya: The limits of regional diplomacy.* Asian Studies Journal, 46(1), 14–31.

126. OCHA. (2019). Funding gaps in the Rohingya response: Challenges in humanitarian aid. Retrieved from https://www.unocha.org

127. Portes, A., & Rumbaut, R. G. (2014). *Immigrant America: A portrait* (4th ed.). University of California Press.

128. Rahman, M. (2018). *The Rohingya crisis: Impact on Bangladesh and beyond.* Routledge.

129. Rashid, M. (2020). *Gender and education among Rohingya refugees in Bangladesh.* Gender and Development, 28(1), 99-112.

130. Ratha, D., De, S., & Mohapatra, S. (2019). Remittances and economic growth: A global perspective. *World Bank Policy Research Working*

Paper, 8969, 1-30.

131. Ratha, D., Mohapatra, S., & Xu, Z. (2016). *Remittances and development: The impact of remittances on economic development.* World Bank.

132. Riley, A., Varner, A., & Bass, J. (2020). Mental health needs among displaced Rohingya: Lessons from the field. *Journal of Global Mental Health, 7*(1), 45-62.

133. Rohingya Blogger. (2017). *The role of social media in the Rohingya crisis.* Rohingya Blogger. https://www.rohingyablogger.org/2017/09/social-media-rohingya-crisis

134. Rohingya Organisation UK. (2014). *The history of the Rohingya people.* https://www.rohingya.org

135. Rothman, S. (2016). *The role of religion in preserving Rohingya identity: A case study of the diaspora in Canada.* Canadian Journal of Muslim Studies, 9(2), 45-61.

136. Saha, K. (2021). Security implications of the Rohingya refugee crisis in South Asia. *South Asian Journal of International Relations, 13*(3), 214-233.

137. Saleh, T., Faisal, M., & Jalil, M. (2020). Environmental stressors caused by refugee settlements: A case study of Bangladesh. *Global Environmental Change, 63,* 102118 https://doi.org/10.1016/j.gloenvcha.2020.102118

138. Sanchez, P. (2020). *The EU's evolving migration policy: Responses to the refugee crisis.* European Politics and Society, 21(3), 255-272.

139. Saxenian, A. (2002). *Brain circulation: How high-skill immigration makes everyone better off.* The Brookings Institution Press.

140. Schain, M. (2021). *Populism, nationalism, and*

migration: A comparative perspective. Political Studies Review, 19(2), 112-130.

141. Schmeidl, S. (2017). *Rethinking refugee status and statelessness in the global era.* Journal of Refugee Studies, 30(1), 1-22.

142. Seng, M. (2017). *The Rohingya: A history of persecution.* The Diplomat. https://www.thediplomat.com

143. Siddique, A., & Omar, F. (2020). *Education and integration: The Rohingya refugee experience in Southeast Asia.* Asian Education Review, 11(3), 209-225.

144. Siddiqui, R. (2021). *Digital activism and advocacy: The role of the Rohingya diaspora on social media.* International Journal of Communication, 15(3), 82-97.

145. Siddiqui, S. (2020). *The role of women in rebuilding communities in the Rohingya refugee camps: A qualitative study.* Journal of Gender Studies, 29(4), 404-416. https://doi.org/10.1080/09589236.2020.1779286

146. Singh, P. (2019). *Urbanization and the demographic changes in South Asia.* Springer.

147. Sultana, R. (2019). *Digital Activism in the Rohingya Diaspora: Social Media and the Struggle for Justice.* Journal of Refugee Studies, 32(4), 592-609.

148. Tan, J. (2017). Understanding the refugee crisis: Lessons from the Rohingya. Asia-Pacific Human Rights Journal, 26(4), 231-245.

149. Tan, J. (2021). Refugee integration in Southeast Asia: Challenges and opportunities. Migration and Development Review, 8(3), 1-18.

150. UNHCR. (2016). The Rohingya Refugee Crisis: An

Overview. United Nations High Commissioner for Refugees.

151. UNHCR. (2017). Rohingya refugee crisis: Emergency response and future solutions. United Nations High Commissioner for Refugees.

152. UNHCR. (2018). Annual Report on Refugee Situations: Bangladesh, Myanmar, and Southeast Asia. United Nations High Commissioner for Refugees.

153. UNHCR. (2018). *Rohingya Emergency.* Retrieved from https://www.unhcr.org

154. UNHCR. (2019). Education in emergencies: Rohingya refugees in Bangladesh. United Nations High Commissioner for Refugees.

155. UNHCR. (2019). *Global Trends: Forced Displacement in 2018*. United Nations High Commissioner for Refugees. Retrieved from https://www.unhcr.org/globaltrends

156. UNHCR. (2019). Global trends: Forced displacement in 2019. *United Nations High Commissioner for Refugees*. Retrieved from https://www.unhcr.org

157. UNHCR. (2019). *Rohingya refugee response: 2019 update*. United Nations High Commissioner for Refugees. https://www.unhcr.org/

158. UNHCR. (2020). *Education in displacement: The challenges of Rohingya youth*. United Nations High Commissioner for Refugees. Retrieved from https://www.unhcr.org/education

159. UNHCR. (2020). Humanitarian aid and long-term displacement: The impact of the Rohingya refugee crisis. United Nations High Commissioner for

Refugees.

160. UNHCR. (2021). *Global report on statelessness.* Retrieved from https://www.unhcr.org/statelessness

161. UNHCR. (2021). Global Trends in Refugee Resettlement: A Case Study of the Rohingya Refugee Crisis. United Nations High Commissioner for Refugees.

162. UNHCR. (2023). *Global trends: Forced displacement in 2022.* United Nations High Commissioner for Refugees. Retrieved from https://www.unhcr.org/global-trends

163. UNICEF. (2020). Rohingya crisis: Maternal and child health at risk. Retrieved from https://www.unicef.org

164. UNICEF. (2021). *Education for displaced youth: A study on Rohingya refugees in Bangladesh.* United Nations Children's Fund. Retrieved from https://www.unicef.org/education

165. United Nations High Commissioner for Human Rights. (2017). *Myanmar: The military's crackdown on the Rohingya.* United Nations. https://www.ohchr.org/en/countries/asia/rohingya-crisis

166. United Nations High Commissioner for Refugees (UNHCR). (1951). *The Convention relating to the Status of Refugees.* UNHCR.

167. United Nations High Commissioner for Refugees (UNHCR). (2017). *Refugee crisis in South Asia: The Rohingya experience.* UNHCR. Retrieved from https://www.unhcr.org/rohingya-crisis

168. United Nations High Commissioner for Refugees

(UNHCR). (2019). *Environmental impacts of refugee camps: A global overview.* UNHCR. https://www.unhcr.org

169. United Nations High Commissioner for Refugees (UNHCR). (2019). *The refugee situation in the Middle East and North Africa.* Retrieved from https://www.unhcr.org.

170. United Nations High Commissioner for Refugees (UNHCR). (2020). *Global trends: Forced displacement in 2020.* United Nations.

171. United Nations High Commissioner for Refugees (UNHCR). (2020). *Rohingya refugees.* https://www.unhcr.org

172. United Nations High Commissioner for Refugees. (2018). *Rohingya refugees: A global overview of the resettlement process.* UNHCR. https://www.unhcr.org

173. WFP. (2019). Nutritional status of Rohingya refugees: Key findings. *World Food Programme.* Retrieved from https://www.wfp.org

174. WHO. (2020). Health and humanitarian crises in refugee camps. World Health Organization.

175. World Bank. (2020). *Urbanization in Southeast Asia.* Retrieved from https://www.worldbank.org

176. World Bank. (2021). Assessing the impact of long-term displacement: Lessons from the Rohingya refugee camps. World Bank Reports.

177. World Bank. (2023). *Population density and urbanization in South Asia.* World Bank. Retrieved from https://www.worldbank.org/population_density

178. World Food Programme. (2020). *Impact of mass*

displacement on host countries: A report on the strain on food security. WFP. https://www.wfp.org

179. World Health Organization. (2018). *Health challenges in refugee camps in Bangladesh.* World Health Organization. https://www.who.int/emergencies/crises/rohingya

180. Yusuf, M. (2017). *The Rohingya of Myanmar: Identity, Persecution, and Refugee Politics.* Asian Journal of Refugee Studies, 14(2), 78-95.

181. Zaman, A., & Samad, F. (2020). The economic impact of the Rohingya crisis on host countries: A regional analysis. Asian Development Review, 33(4), 204-220.

182. Zin, N. (2019). *Rohingya Refugees in Malaysia: Challenges and Prospects. Asian Journal of Social Science,* 47(2), 123–143.